fifty
SOMERSET
CHURCHES

fifty
SOMERSET
CHURCHES

⌘

ROBERT DUNNING

Somerset Books

First Published in Great Britain in 1996 by Somerset Books

British Library Cataloguing in Publication Data

Data for this publication is available from the British Library

ISBN 0 86183 309 0

SOMERSET BOOKS
Official Publisher to Somerset County Council

Halsgrove House
Lower Moor Way
Tiverton EX16 6SS
Tel: 01884 243242
Fax 01884 243325

Printed and bound in Great Britain by Longdunn Press Ltd

Contents

Dedication

To those who in the past built to the glory of God; to those who in the present have still not lost faith in maintaining them; and to John Bickersteth, sometime bishop of Bath and Wells, with whom more than once the author helped to save a threatened building.

Foreword

by the Lord Bishop of Bath and Wells,
The Right Reverend James Thompson

'This is the most beautiful church in Somerset'. I don't know how many times I have been told that but one of the privileges of the Bishop of Bath and Wells is to visit so many of the wondrous collection of churches in the diocese. Dr Dunning's book about 50 of those churches is a sheer delight. He not only presents us with the history of the churches but we also learn about the people who have made them what they are, about the communities in which they are set and about their life throught the ages. Great care has been taken in the research and there are many moving and entertaining stories here which I suspect might well feature in future sermons of the Bishops of Bath and Wells.

I had not thought that I would find a book about church buildings to be all that encouraging to my faith, but in this chronicle there is so much to encourage us – the essential relationship over the centuries between church and community; the dedication of small groups of people and individuals to keep their village church going against all odds; the never ending resilience in the battle for funds and the joy and fun of all the fêtes and shows and gymkhanas organised to raise them; but perhaps, above all, the continuing desire to worship God in a place set apart for that purpose, to remind us of the God who is in and through all things.

It is understandable that there should only be 50 churches included in this book because 580 plus would make some volume, but I can't but help look forward to the next 50.

There is I believe a growing spiritual hunger in our land and that is partly expressed by the desire to explore our history because we feel we need to rediscover our roots in a very rootless society. There are few places more illuminating to look than in the churches of England.

Acknowledgements

D r Joseph Bettey read the whole manuscript and offered helpful corrections and additions; Dr John Harvey gave me copies of his notes on dating materials and on the medieval accounts of the Wells chapter estates; the Very Revd Dom Philip Jebb, prior and archivist of Downside Abbey, gave me access to the archives of St Benedict's, Stratton on the Fosse. The Ven. Richard Acworth, archdeacon of Wells, Jenny Aish of Angersleigh, Jane Barbour of Winchester, John Kinross of Burrowbridge, John Holmes of Kingston St Mary and my colleague Mary Siraut gave me answers to particular questions. At every turn David Bromwich has been a great support. I am grateful to Steven Pugsley for being enthusiastic about publishing this book when it was only a title and to David Cawthorne for including it among the County Council's Library Service publications. Readers will see clearly how much is owed to the photographic skills of Bob Winn. Clergy, churchwardens and other officers have willingly given access to churches and chapels in their care. This book is, in a real sense, a record of what they and their predecessors have done in building, restoring, preserving and maintaining places of Christian worship in one diocese and county.

Most of the illustrations are the work of Bob Winn, specially commissioned for this book. Acknowledgement of other illustrations is made as follows. Author: 20 (by Abbot Horne), 183, and cover pictures; Downside Abbey: 182; Peter Leach: vii; Philip Nokes: 186; Somerset Archaeological and Natural History Society: 16 (by T.H. Smith), 22 (by J. Buckler), 36 (by J. Buckler), 48, 152 (by J. Buckler); Somerset Record Office: 158; Somerset Studies Library, 116, 123, 125, 129, 137, 153, 160, 164, 169 (by J.W. Brett), 172.

Abbreviations

P.R.O.	Public Record Office
Proc. Som. Arch. Soc.	*Proceedings of the Somersetshire Archaeological and Natural History Society*
S.D.N.Q.	*Somerset and Dorset Notes and Queries*
S.R.O.	Somerset Record Office
S.R.S.	Somerset Record Society
V.C.H.	*Victoria County History of Somerset*

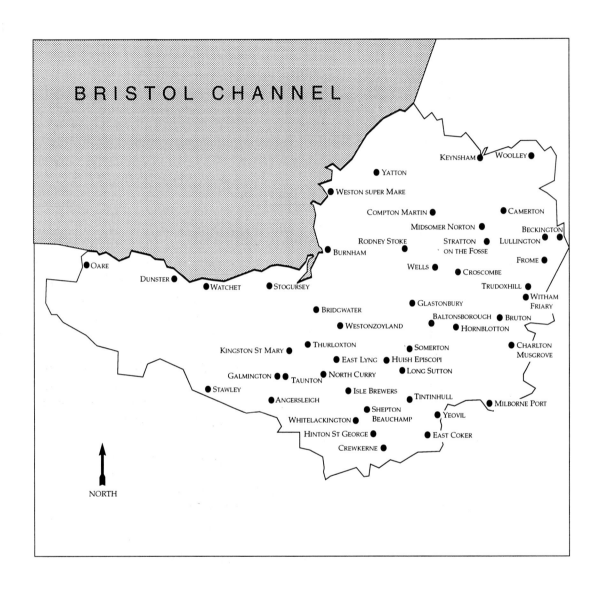

BRISTOL CHANNEL

KEYNSHAM ● ● WOOLLEY

● YATTON

● WESTON SUPER MARE

COMPTON MARTIN ● ● CAMERTON

MIDSOMER NORTON ●

RODNEY STOKE ● STRATTON ● LULLINGTON ● BECKINGTON

ON THE FOSSE ● FROME

● OARE ● BURNHAM WELLS ● ● CROSCOMBE

DUNSTER ● TRUDOXHILL ●

● WATCHET ● STOGURSEY ● WITHAM
FRIARY

● GLASTONBURY

● BRIDGWATER BALTONSBOROUGH ● ● BRUTON

● WESTONZOYLAND ● HORNBLOTTON

KINGSTON ST MARY ● ● THURLOXTON ● SOMERTON ● CHARLTON
MUSGROVE

● EAST LYNG ● HUISH EPISCOPI

GALMINGTON ● ● ● LONG SUTTON

TAUNTON ● NORTH CURRY ● MILBORNE PORT

● STAWLEY ● ISLE BREWERS

● TINTINHULL

● ANGERSLEIGH

● SHEPTON
BEAUCHAMP ● YEOVIL

WHITELACKINGTON ●

HINTON ST GEORGE ● ● EAST COKER

CREWKERNE ●

↑

NORTH

Introduction

In 1991 when George Carey left Wells to become the 103rd archbishop of Canterbury in succession to St Augustine he was presented with a pectoral cross made in the image and likeness of one which had then recently been found near Shepton Mallet. A copy of the same cross was later given by the diocese to Bishop Basil Sambano of Dar es Salaam, whose own see has for some years been linked with the rural deanery of Taunton. For the new archbishop, the gift was a reminder that Christianity was thriving in Somerset in the fourth or fifth century; for Bishop Basil it is an ancient symbol of the Faith his people have held for little more than a century.

The significance of the Shepton Mallet cross, or rather amulet, is that it is decorated with a Chi Rho symbol. It was found in a grave in a small cemetery of east-west burials and may well have belonged to the priest of a small Christian community, evidently a minority, in an otherwise pagan settlement beside the Fosse Way. The amulet, dating to about 500 AD, may be the latest datable object so far found there and the little group of Christians may have been the last inhabitants, making a living from the dwindling traffic passing between the once thriving cities of Bath and Exeter.

It is unlikely that Shepton had the only Christian community; unlikely that among the many visitors to Bath during the time of the Roman occupation there were not Christians from some distant part of the Empire. Who knows what official or soldier from Rome stationed in this part of the province of Britannia had not seen or heard Peter or Paul back home ? And how soon was the message of the apostles brought across the western sea ? The more extreme claims of Glastonbury to be the cradle of Christianity in the West are unhistorical, but among the traders between the eastern Mediterranean and Cornwall, long before the coming of St Augustine, there may well have been men nurtured in the Faith. St Augustine's own visit to the West of England at the beginning of the seventh century was to meet leaders of a church which had been so long settled in the region as to have developed its own traditions and an organisation singularly adapted to the social and geographical characteristics of the Celtic world.

Celtic traditions grew in a countryside of scattered settlement where leadership was found in monastic communities; Augustine's experience was in an essentially urban-based church, where the parochial unit had obvious secular parallels. The parish in Wessex developed gradually within the context of Saxon conquest from the late seventh century, the time of King Ine onwards. The parish church is thus not the earliest Christian phenomenon in what came to be Somerset, and relatively few such churches have even fragments dating from the period before the Norman Conquest. But the well-founded presence of Celtic saints along the coast of West Somerset and the remarkable achievements of Aldhelm in the east are so firmly linked with the present parish churches of St Decuman, Porlock or Timberscombe on the one hand and of Frome, Bruton or Doulting on the other, that this study of fifty churches stands for the authentic history of Christianity in the heart of Wessex from its traceable beginnings to the present day.

P. Leach, *Shepton Mallet: Romano-Britons and Early Christians in Somerset.*

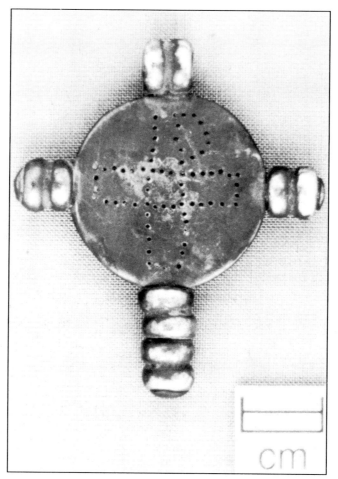

Early Christian cross from Shepton Mallet

The Celtic Mission
WATCHET, *St Decuman*

~⚜~

The tall, rather gaunt tower of St Decuman's church stands isolated on the end of the ridge overlooking the little port of Watchet, a fine site from which to survey its parish but hardly a sensible one to encourage church attendance. Yet the name of the patron saint and the choice of the site lie at the very heart of the history of the mission of the Celtic Church along the coast from West Somerset to Cornwall in the years after the removal of the Roman armies from Britain.

Decuman is a name derived from the Latin word associated with tax collection. The saint probably came from West Wales where the church of Rhoscrowther, five miles west of Pembroke, is also known as Llanddegyman or Eglwys Degeman, Decuman's church. In the tenth century this was one of the ten churches in Dyfed headed by a scholar abbot-bishop. A church near Rhoscrowther, another in Brecon and a chapel in

Watchet: *St Decuman's church and the Bristol Channel*

St Wendron parish in Cornwall all bear his name, a measure of his importance in the Celtic Church. His death is recorded as 706 AD.

The 'Life' of the saint compiled in the fifteenth century tells what little is known of Decuman's activities in Somerset. He came across from Wales on a hurdle (or perhaps in a coracle) and lived as a hermit sustained by the milk of a cow. One day while he was at prayer a pagan cut off the top of his head but he took up the severed part and carried it to his well. That was enough to establish sanctity and in the fifteenth century his feast was kept with due solemnity both at Wells cathedral and at Muchelney abbey on 27 August.

But there was another feast associated with the saint. In 1412, to settle a dispute with the people of Williton, the vicar of St Decuman's promised to appoint and pay a chaplain for Williton (the vicar is still the patron of the living). In return, Williton people agreed to attend services at St Decuman's and to make offerings there on four special feasts: St Decuman's day, All Saints' day (the Dedication day of Williton), Ascension day and the feast of the Translation of St Decuman. That last is a date which is quite unknown, for no such feast occurs in any church calendar, but the removal of his bones from one resting place to another makes some sense of the odd site of the parish church.

Watchet: *Wyndham family memorials*

Watchet: *interior*

Across the valley and now teetering on the edge of the cliff are some earthworks known in the sixteenth century as Le Castell and since then as Daw's Castle after a tenant who farmed the land. Archaeologists have found traces of Roman and perhaps of earlier settlement there but its importance came when in the early tenth century a fort was built there forming part of a chain to defend the land against Viking raids. Just outside the fort lay a field later known as Old Minster, a name recalling the site of an ancient church.

It was probably this church, perhaps a Celtic foundation, which was first established in the name of Decuman. The sea evidently began to threaten, as it has continued to do, and the wise decision was taken to move the church, and with it Decuman's bones. Hence the translation. No part of the present building is earlier than the late thirteenth century, the date of the long and unusually wide chancel, perhaps built especially to house a shrine with the saint's bones.

The remainder of the church was rebuilt in the fifteenth or the early sixteenth century, probably in several stages to judge from the three different styles seen in the nave arcades, possibly because there was once a central tower. The north aisle and north chapel are of one date, later than the west tower; the south aisle had a chapel at its east end before the building of the south chancel chapel. Tell-tale scars in the pillars of the nave suggest that chapels were formed by the rood screen and parcloses, probably in both aisles and nave. Crudely carved figures of St Anthony and St George survive in niches in the north arcade. In the mid fourteenth century a parishioner left money for lights of St Decuman, the Virgin Mary, St Nicholas, St Peter, St James and the High Cross and wax for the silver candle before the image of St Decuman. Around these lights or images some of the chapels must have been formed.

The north chancel chapel has for long been the private chapel of the Wyndhams of Orchard Wyndham and contains the family pew installed in 1688 and memorials to various members of this most distinguished family. What was once the most impressive tomb, that of Sir John Wyndham (died 1574) has now lost its canopy, a former vicar having found its parlous state too alarming to contemplate and too expensive to repair. John Wyndham (died 1645) and his wife are commemorated by portrait busts which may well be by Nicholas Stone, and John's son William (died 1683), remembered as a healer of wounds after the Civil War, evidently deserved the memorial of the finest quality which bears his name and high praises.

V.C.H. Somerset v. 146, 165–8; D. H. Farmer, *The Oxford Dictionary of Saints; Proc. Som. Arch. Soc.* cxxx. 47–60.

St Aldhem and the Roman Church
BRUTON, *St Mary*

～✕～

Every seven miles between Doulting, where he had died, and Malmesbury, where he was to be buried, a stone cross was erected to mark the route taken by a procession bearing the body of St Aldhelm in the year 709, just three years after the death of St Decuman. Aldhelm was himself a product of the Celtic Mission but, as bishop of Sherborne and thus of the whole of Saxon-conquered Somerset from 705, he was also the representative of the Roman tradition as introduced through Canterbury by St Augustine a little more than a century earlier. He represents in his own ministry the healing of the breach between the two traditions which Augustine himself rather widened than narrowed when about 603 he met the leaders of the British, Celtic Church on the West Saxon border at Augustine's Oak.

Aldhelm, the subject of at least five 'Lives' of which only two survive from the late twelfth and the early thirteenth centuries, was born at Wareham perhaps about 640 of a landed family, related in some way to the Saxon king Cynegils, himself converted to Christianity by St Birinus in 635. Aldhelm was educated at Malmesbury by an Irish pilgrim scholar Maildulf. He later moved to Canterbury for more advanced study in a school which had been set up by Archbishop Theodore of Tarsus and was in his time under Abbot Hadrian from North Africa. Aldhelm thus came for the first time into direct contact with the Roman tradition. About 672 he had to leave Canterbury because of ill health and presumably returned to Malmesbury where, three years later, he was chosen abbot. Back home, where as a young monk he had taken his lyre down to the river to sing ballads, he returned to his Celtic roots, to a monastery still in touch with the British kingdom in the South-West but taking its place within the Saxon territorial see under the leadership of Hlothere, bishop of the West Saxons based at Winchester.

In the Celtic tradition, where leadership was vested in abbots rather than in bishops, Aldhelm built two churches at Malmesbury in addition to Maildulf's basilica, founded a religious community at Frome before 701 and another at Bradford on Avon before 705. But he lived in a see which had long accepted the Roman tradition, and on behalf of its synod he wrote to King Geraint of Dumnonia complaining of the treatment Saxons, both clergy and laity, were receiving at the hands of Celtic clergy in South Wales. The letter then became a general treatise taking up St Augustine's arguments for a unifiom date for Easter and other Roman traditions.

Meanwhile the Saxons continued to advance westwards, reaching Taunton c. 682. The West Saxon see had by this time become of unmanageable size and Aldhelm, who had clearly become the leading figure in its western area, was the obvious candidate for

Bruton: *west tower*

bishop when the see was divided. From 705 until his death in 709 Aldhelm was bishop of Sherborne, Father-in-God of the people west of Selwood.

Almost as if in preparation for his appointment, Aldhelm visited Rome in the 690s. From there he brought a marble altar which eventually found its way to Bruton. Aldhelm's writings, in a style peculiarly his own, included ballads which later attracted the attention of King Alfred and riddles which owe a good deal to the work of Isidore of Seville. Bede knew of his 'excellent book' *On Virginity*. The magnificent funeral arranged by Bishop Ecgwin of Worcester was a tribute not only to the close friendship of the two men but of the affection in which the 'Apostle of Selwood' was held.

The tradition recorded in the earlier twelfth century by William of Malmesbury declared that Bruton had two churches, one founded by Ine, king of Wessex, and dedicated to the Virgin Mary; the other, founded by Aldhelm, dedicated to St Peter. Still in William's time St Mary's had the white marble altar which Aldhelm had brought back from Rome and given to King Ine. The altar itself was remarkable: six feet thick, four feet long and two palms broad, its projecting lip beautifully carved. It was said that a camel had borne it as far as the Alps. Both the camel's back and the altar had been broken and although Aldhelm miraculously mended both, the altar still bore the scars.

Aldhelm's church, it seems likely, survived in altered form to become the church of a religious community founded, so John Leland recorded, by Algar, earl of Cornwall, at the beginning of the eleventh century. That same building, or its successor, became the church of the priory founded in 1142. It was then still dedicated to St Mary and St Aldhelm.

In the earlier twelfth century there was also 'another great church' whose east front had been 'lately enlarged'. It was quite separate from the priory church and Leland in the early sixteenth century wrote of 'the paroche chirch and thabbay by it' standing beyond the river from the town. Pevsner calls the parish church 'one of the proudest', Francis Eeles the 'finest', Kenneth Wickham the 'noblest' in East Somerset. The church was, in strict ecclesiastical law, a chapel, dependent upon its mother, the priory church. In 1446 it was said to be dedicated to St Katherine and 'commonly called the parish church'. Bruton in the later Middle Ages was a prosperous place and its merchants clearly wanted to make the most of their building and were not likely to let such a small matter as legal dependence come between them and their desire to display their religious devotion.

The crypt under the chancel, of the early fourteenth century and the oldest part of the present church, must have been formed at the same time as a new chancel above it, replacing who knows what building but presumably the new work mentioned in the earlier twelfth century. Later in the fourteenth century a north aisle was added to an existing nave and a porch-tower to the aisle. The next stage was to rebuild the nave, which later had a rood screen across the chancel arch and two screens further west in the aisles to create four other chapels.

Bruton: *eighteenth-century chancel beyond twentieth-century screen*

Wills in the fifteenth century refer to the high altar and to altars of Our Lady and Holy Cross, to images of St Katherine and St Mary Magdalene, to the rood, and in 1500 and 1509 to work proceeding on a new Lady Chapel, evidently financed by a fraternity of Our Lady which had been founded some thirty years or more earlier.

The last significant addition to the medieval building was the west tower. It is considered to be the design of a mason near 1450, but it is not likely to have been completed until after 1485 and probably before 1490. Other building works were mentioned in a will of 1471 and Alice Brymmore in 1516 left money for the 'new building' of the south aisle, work still progressing in 1520. That was probably followed by more work on the nave where the clerestory was formed and a new roof made. The construction of its parapets and those of both aisles may be dated as a whole by the shields and monograms on the north parapet where the mitre and dolphin of Richard FitzJames, bishop of London 1506–22, and the initials of William Gilbert, prior and later abbot of Bruton 1494–1533, and of Richard Bere, abbot of Glastonbury 1494–1525, put the date of the work early in the sixteenth century and suggest how the operation was financed.

The final significant addition strikes the visitor on entering. The medieval chancel was rebuilt in 1743 by the patron Sir Charles Berkeley in the contemporary Classical style which provides such a contrast to the Gothic of the rest of the building. Restoration in 1869–70 almost destroyed this restrained Baroque elegance in favour of Victorian Gothic, and the present chancel screen of 1938 succeeds in continuing the style in a more modern idiom. An earlier screen in the tower arch, largely of 1620 but incorporating fragments of a fifteenth-century rood screen, would appear to have been its too-heavy predecessor. Other survivals from the time of the priory are some fragments of glass in two clerestory windows, parts of a late-medieval altar frontal with the monogram of William Gilbert, and the same initials and the FitzJames dolphin on the fourth bell with the date 1528.

Almost nothing survives above ground of the great priory, made an abbey in 1511, which after its dissolution in 1539 was bought by the Berkeley family and converted to a mansion. The mansion itself was destroyed by fire, rebuilt, abandoned and in the late 1780s demolished, leaving a level site which makes a fine cricket pitch for the school begun in or before 1515. That school, firmly established by Abbot Gilbert and a prominent member of the FitzJames family, has almost adopted the north aisle of the present parish church, where memorials to many masters and pupils serve as a reminder of the ancient link between church and abbey which would have delighted St Aldhelm's heart.

H.M. Porter, *Saint Aldhelm, Abbot and Bishop*; *William of Malmesbury, Gesta Pontificum*, 374; *Proc. Som. Arch Soc.* lxxix. 1–18; *V.C.H. Somerset* vii (forthcoming).

King Alfred and the Revival of the Faith
LYNG, *St Bartholomew* and
BURROW, *St Michael*

~❧~

> And I would have it known that very often it has come
> to my mind what men of learning there were formerly
> throughout England, both in religious and secular
> orders ... and how they [the kings] succeeded both in
> warfare and in wisdom; and also how eager were the
> religious orders both in teaching and in learning as
> well as in all the holy services which it was their
> duty to perform for God ... and how nowadays, if we
> wished to acquire these things, we would have to seek
> them outside. Learning had declined so thoroughly in
> England that there were very few men on this side of
> the Humber who could understand their divine services
> in English ...
>
> (Trans. S. Keynes and M. Lapidge)

With these words King Alfred introduced his translation of Pope Gregory's *Pastoral Care*, a work directed to the holders of ecclesiastical office and which the king designed for distribution to the bishops of his realm.

Alfred's reference to the decline of learning was written with some feeling. When he planned his monastery at Athelney he had been unable to find either noble or freeborn Englishmen willing to undertake the monastic life. Asser, Alfred's biographer, declared that monasteries founded in the neighbourhood earlier, presumably Glastonbury and Muchelney, no longer maintained a monastic rule 'in any consistent way' because of enemy attacks and because life outside the cloister was too comfortable.

The first monks at Athelney, therefore, were foreigners, led by John the Old Saxon and including men from Gaul and one of Viking origin. The new community, housed on the remote 'island' in the marshes where the king himself had found refuge when the Viking armies were overwhelming the West, was established about 886 and was designed, like its sister foundation at Shaftesbury under the rule of Alfred's daughter Aethelgifu, to lead the revival of the Church in Wessex. As a monastic community it was probably never distinguished, but as the creation of King Alfred it was part of the king's programme to re-establish the Church in the countryside.

Lyng: *St Bartholomew's*

Not far away from Athelney the Alfred Jewel was found at the end of the seventeenth century. Modern scholars believe it was probably the handle of a pointer, one of a number each given to a bishop with a copy of the king's translation of *Pastoral Care* both as a sign of the great importance Alfred attached to the work and as a graphic means of teaching. Athelney's own mission was as much to provide educated men for the priesthood as to revive monastic life in the land. The later fame of St Dunstan and Glastonbury probably put Athelney's contribution in the shade, and its own immediate 'parish' was not huge, like those of Crewkerne or Keynsham, and was largely confined to the marshland where the rivers Parrett, Cary and Tone met. How soon it is not possible to say, but chapels were built on two nearby 'islands' so that their inhabitants might hear divine service as King Alfred would have wished.

Both chapels were in existence when Pope Innocent IV confirmed the possessions of Athelney abbey in 1245, and were then described as the chapels of Lenga and Burgo, that is [East] Lyng, built on the post-Alfredian defences of the fortress there and still possessing a twelfth-century font, and Burrow Mump, where early twelfth-century remains may represent some kind of beacon to serve traders using the Parrett. By the middle of the fourteenth century a permanent income had been arranged for the chaplain at Lyng, but not until 1403 was a parish created. In that year the abbot of Athelney made a formal agreement with the vicar, John Hobbaa (sic), and a group of Lyng people – William Cote, John Baker, Henry Colyns, Thomas Bebyl, John Clerk and Peter Ayleward – whereby their chapel became a parish church with all the legal rights which that implied, including the right to have their own burial ground. St Michael's on the Mump remained a chapel.

With legal rights came responsibilities, namely how to find the money to repair the building themselves rather than turning to the abbot as before. Evidently a parish squabble had broken out and in 1444 Abbot John found himself acting as arbitrator. His decision was that, since most of the money would be raised from the sale of an annual brew of ale, the three communities of East Lyng, West Lyng and Burrow, together constituting the parish of East Lyng, should agree solemnly together that the ale should be made jointly by a man from East Lyng and a man from West Lyng. Further, it should be made in a single vat owned by them all which was to be secured with three locks whose keys were to be held by three men appointed by the abbot. Had the three communities tried to take more than their fair share of the proceeds ?

The money thus raised during the later Middle Ages presumably went towards the new building of Burrow chapel, now visible only in an eighteenth-century drawing, and in the tower, windows, screen, pulpit and unusual bench ends at Lyng. The dissolution of Athelney abbey in 1539 made little difference to either church or chapel, but Burrow was commandeered by the army both during the Civil War and Monmouth's Rebellion and in the eighteenth century an attempt to replace the chapel foundered for lack of funds, leaving the unfinished structure for the confusion of visitors. St Bartholomew's, East Lyng, took the former abbey's site within its parish and for three centuries

Burrow: *St Michael's chapel, Burrow Mump, 1763*

continued the abbey's role as the mother church of the marshlands. Successful drainage brought an increase in population along the banks of the Parrett, and the chapel on the Mump was replaced in 1836–7 by a new church at the foot of the hill which was constituted a parish church in 1840. In the 1850s and 1860s it was again linked with Lyng under the same vicar, and in the 1960s and early 1970s shared a vicar with Northmoor Green. Since 1978 both Burrowbridge (as it is now called) and Lyng have been held with Stoke St Gregory, the neighbour to the south, forming a benefice much larger than the medieval abbots of Athelney had in the marshlands but in a grouping which in its essentials can be traced back to the ideas of King Alfred.

V.C.H. Somerset vi. 53–64; *English Historical Documents* i. 888; *Proc. Som. Arch. Soc.* cxxxiii. 111–16; S.R.O. DD/TB 20/4 (eighteenth-century calendar of the first part of the missing cartulary of Athelney abbey).

The Saxon Mission in the Countryside
CREWKERNE, *St Bartholomew*

The cathedral-like church standing above the bustling little town is an architectural gem which seems to owe something of its style to a designer with royal, or at least London, connections. Like that of its neighbour Ilminster, the nave stands high and wide and the north transept seems to be more glass than stone. The two churches share another characteristic: both in origin may be traced back to the beginnings of Christianity in Saxon Wessex, and the richness of the fabric of both is one consequence.

The story of Crewkerne's origins is to be found in documents both ancient and nearly modern: in a Saxon will, in Domesday Book, in complicated legal agreements, in odd traditions and in maps. The will, that of King Alfred, mentions the royal estate at Crewkerne, an estate which was the centre of a hundred of the same name by the time of the Norman Conquest and of a deanery by the late thirteenth century. By 1086 the church of that royal estate, and a large amount of land to support it, had been given by William the Conqueror to his favourite monastery, the abbey of St Stephen in Caen.

Among the legal documents is one, probably belonging to the later thirteenth century, which describes the way in which people in different parts of the parish stood in relation to their parish church. Some paid all their tithes and offerings to the parish church. Those living in Misterton paid some to their own rector but most to the parish church. On one day in the year, the feast of its dedication, they had to go to Crewkerne for absolution and when they died were taken there for burial. There were similar arrangements for the people of Seaborough, Wayford, Oathill, Ashcombe, Bere and Henley and the whole document may have been drawn up because an agreement had just been reached with Eastham.

That agreement, the three clergymen who between them served Crewkerne, and the name Misterton reveal three important characteristics of the conversion of the pagan countryside in the early years of the Saxon occupation. Christian Saxons advancing west established churches, usually at first on royal estates, which became centres of mission staffed by small communities of priests and became known as minsters. As the Faith spread, 'daughter' churches were built to serve smaller communities, some of which, like Seaborough, later became, or sought to become, parish churches in their own right. Some others, like Eastham, Misterton (meaning 'the tun of the minster') and Wayford only managed partial independence for centuries. Not until 1791 did Misterton have its own burial ground, and 'tribute money' of 4d was still offered at the 'mother' church with the church door key each year until 1829.

Crewkerne: *west front*

Crewkerne: *interior, early nineteenth century*

The map, drawn in the 1770s, shows the land, houses and other properties which had earlier been part of the endowment of Crewkerne church, the property once held by St Stephen's, Caen. By the end of the thirteenth century that land was shared between three portioners or rectors, each with a house near the church, forming a kind of small close, and land stretching from the churchyard to the town's market place. Each of the rectors was well paid and the livings attracted distinguished men at the end of the Middle Ages. One was Richard Surland (1479–1509), also subdean of the Chapel Royal and thus a member of the royal household. He was followed by Christopher Plummer (1509–c.1536), chaplain successively to Queen Elizabeth of York, Henry VIII and Catherine of Aragon.

The splendour of the nave and west front includes detailing, panelling and tracery characteristic of William Smyth, mason in charge at Wells Cathedral, Sherborne and Milton abbeys and St John's, Glastonbury. The turrets of the west front perhaps have a different origin, for they recall both Bath abbey and the Tudor royal chapels, the work of Robert and William Vertue.

The square nave, providing space for processions as well as congregations, came to be the ideal shape for the preaching house which the church became after the Reformation. By the end of the sixteenth century music was also important. An organ maker who lived in the town in 1567 may have built an instrument for the church but money for another was left in 1591 'to the setting up of the organs ... if they shall be set up in the honour of Almighty God'. Among the burials recorded were those of singing men in 1585 and 1627. A stricter generation did not care for such frivolities and in 1646 the organ was dismantled. Lead from the bellows, metal from the pipes and the wooden case were listed among the parish lumber. The schoolmaster later leased the organ loft where he set up seats for himself and his pupils.

For two centuries and more the nave was a great preaching arena. In 1809-11 it was re-pewed and galleries were added at the east ends of both aisles; a fine organ in the west gallery effectively blocked the light from the great window. The new pews were of the 'high, straight-backed, horse-stall order', and the music in the 1860s was open to criticism. The choir was 'anything but first-class' and the new organ did not impress a contributor to the *Western Gazette*.

It is possible that practice with the new organ may
in time render it more efficient. Of the organ, I
can only say that I like its sounds much better than
I do its appearance ... my impression is, that it
was designed by somebody who never saw the church.

Work in the 1880s and at the turn of the century restored the church's fine medieval
proportions and prepared the way for the revival of some of the liturgical traditions of an
earlier age. Striking additions of the mid 1980s are colourful banners recalling the families associated with the church in the early Middle Ages, including the three roundels of
the Courtenays, lords of the manor of Crewkerne from the thirteenth century until the
sixteenth and patrons of each of the three portions from 1315 until 1547.

V.C.H. Somerset iv. 28–34; *Proc. Som. Arch. Soc.* cxx. 63–7; *English Historical Documents*, i. 534–7.

Scholar, Craftsman, Statesman and Saint
BALTONSBOROUGH, *St Dunstan*

'Perp and of no special architectural interest', says Pevsner; but there is more interest than architecture, and the dedication of the church to St Dunstan is a reminder that the village was probably the birthplace of one of Somerset's most famous sons.

The reforms of church government begun by King Alfred and continued by 'the wise and venerable' Archbishop Plegmund of Canterbury included the division of the two Wessex bishoprics of Winchester and Sherborne and the creation of five new ones including Wells, whose first bishop, Athelm, was Dunstan's uncle. The year of the foundation of the diocese of Wells, 909, was probably the year of Dunstan's birth. His parents were Heorstan and Cynethrith, owners of land and members of a distinguished family which included besides Athelm, bishops Alphege of Winchester and Kinsige of Lichfield and others in secular life at the court of King Athelstan. The family might have been connected, like Aldhelm's, with the royal line and Dunstan's latest biographer, Douglas Dales, even speculates that Dunstan's forebears 'may have been among the immediate retinue of Alfred when he was based at Athelney ... in the winter of 878'.

Dunstan's subsequent eminence gave rise to a number of 'Lives' which included semi-miraculous stories beginning with the appearance of fire to his pregnant mother at a Candlemas service. More realistic are the claims for his education at Glastonbury, then still strongly under Irish Celtic influence and possibly a religious community under secular rule.

The boy became a man. Taking minor clerical orders, perhaps at Glastonbury, he first followed his uncle Athelm to Canterbury and then entered the cultured court of Athelstan, Alfred's grandson, often to be found at Cheddar. At court the learned and spiritual youth provoked opposition from his contemporaries and even possibly from some of his own kinsfolk. Under some pressure from Alphege, recently made bishop of Winchester, Dunstan and another youth named Ethelwold were both tonsured as monks and joined the bishop's household, itself distinguished for its regular and ascetic life in the midst of many worldly clergy.

Among the many stories told of the young Dunstan is that of the appearance of the Devil in his workshop. It is, perhaps, to be associated with the saint's frequent journeys back to Glastonbury to visit the hermit-widow Aethelfleda, who became his spiritual mother and deepened his experience of the religious life. Metal-working, harp-playing, writing, painting and designing were all recalled later as the achievements of a man who clearly had to struggle hard to overcome the temptations his privileged background offered.

Baltonsborough: *St Dunstan's church*

Athelstan died in 939 and Dunstan returned to serve the new king, Edmund. Again he fell foul of court intrigue and was threatened with exile, but the king's miraculous escape from death in Cheddar Gorge produced a dramatic change of heart and Dunstan found himself appointed abbot of Glastonbury in 942 or 943. From that time the abbey became the focus of interest of the king and his court, and with such endowments Dunstan was able to build extensively, providing both a centre of pilgrimage and enclosed monastic quarters where the Rule of St Benedict might be properly followed. But it was far more than an impressive collection of buildings, a wealthy centre of learning and religious life. Dunstan the 'athlete of God' made Glastonbury a school of prayer with enormous influence. 'By his care, holy religious life emerged there, and ... was spread by Dunstan from that place throughout the whole world of the English.'

During the late 940s and 950s Dunstan remained abbot but was still very close to the court and to King Eadred, twice refusing to be a bishop. He was forced into exile in 956 and at Ghent came into contact with monastic reform movements in Flanders. A year later he returned at the invitation of Edgar, then ruler of a divided kingdom, and probably in the next year Dunstan was consecrated bishop, to serve at court rather than in a territorial see, although he was later named bishop of Worcester and for a short time also of London. In 959 Edgar became ruler of a united kingdom and within a month he had removed the recently appointed archbishop of Canterbury and appointed Dunstan in his stead.

For nearly thirty years Dunstan ruled at Canterbury, and for just over half of those his close relationship with the young King Edgar was a formidable combination. Edgar's coronation at Bath in 973 when the king had reached the age of 30, the canonical age for consecration, marked in its powerful symbolism both the sacred character of kingship and the personal influence of Dunstan and his fellow monastic reformers, notably Ethelwold of Winchester. The solemn ceremony in a sense marked the end of their work, for behind the king were laws which gave the Church a position of privilege, and behind Dunstan and his fellow monks was the *Regularis Concordia*, the formal agreement between the monasteries of the land as to how the great Rule of St Benedict was to be nationally observed.

Dunstan lived another thirteen years after the early death of Edgar. They were years of political turmoil in which, nevertheless, Edgar's laws and Dunstan's reforms proved crucial to the survival of the state. Dunstan the pastor and teacher spent his later days in his diocese, still in contact with the continental reformers but essentially the contemplative monk-bishop. Early on the morning of 19 May 988 he died, surrounded by the

Glastonbury abbey: *excavations of St Dunstan's church, 1928*

monastic community he had ruled for so long. Within ten years of his death he was being called a saint.

How soon the church of his native place received his name will probably never be known. In strict ecclesiastical law it was a chapelry of Butleigh, and thus evidently later in foundation. And it is certainly not without interest, if only because chancel, nave, west tower, south porch and door, benches, font and pulpit all seem to be of one period. Also of interest is the unusually wide nave, which has brought with it problems of stress in the roof and an alarming outward lean of the north wall. The wagon vault of the nave with its rich ceilure at the east end to cover the former rood loft, and the richly carved wall plates of the chancel are worth a second look. So is the (alas now empty) hour-glass holder near the preacher's hand. The fine screen was designed by Frederick Bligh Bond, a great student of Glastonbury and its abbey; the contemporary choir stalls, since the Tractarian revival the essential furnishing of every chancel, hark back here most appropriately to their monastic forebears.

D. Dales, *Dunstan: Saint and Statesman.*

A Domesday Church
MILBORNE PORT,
St John the Evangelist

Domesday Book records (among many other things) the riches of the Church in the late eleventh century, or rather the riches of some influential bishops and the estates of monastic houses. There are not many parish churches mentioned, even fewer parish clergy. Among the most remarkable at the time must have been Regenbald or Reinbald, a powerful member of the court of Edward the Confessor and dean of the rich college at Cirencester. In Somerset in the Conqueror's survey he held the valuable minster church at Frome and the church of the large royal estate of Milborne.

Milborne church was a minster; its original 'parish' reached well into what is now Dorset and represented a centre of mission established in the early years of the Saxon conquest, probably by the early eighth century before county boundaries were fixed. Such a claim can be inferred from documents later possessed by Cirencester abbey which was

Milborne Port: *chancel and south transept, 1839*

Milborne Port: *interior showing crossing*

founded by Henry I after the death of Regenbald and endowed with his lands. Cirencester owned Milborne church and appointed its clergy until the Dissolution in 1539.

Domesday Book declares that with his church at Milborne Regenbald held a hide of land, perhaps as many as 120 acres of arable. This large holding reflected, of course, the central role of a mother church. By the time of Domesday some of its 'daughters' had probably achieved independence, although by then Milborne was a busy place where a small town had grown up around a market (hence the later additional name Port), a place where up to thirty years before the Conquest a mint had operated. By 1086 there were several water mills nearby and some 100 families working the surrounding land.

The present parish church, standing in a large churchyard away from the noise of the A30, is a building which has often featured in books on Romanesque architecture though experts are not agreed whether its main feature, the central crossing, belongs to the period just before or just after the Conquest. Since Regenbald spans both there is a fair assumption that the work is associated with him, and that work is of the highest quality, still to be appreciated despite attempts by Victorian restorers to improve it.

Indeed, the fabric of the church actually reflects very well the economic fortunes of the town which it served and the people who supported it. Late Saxon and early-Norman prosperity may be recognised in the south wall of the chancel, decorated in a manner recalling St Laurence's at Bradford on Avon. The lower stage of the great crossing tower and the south transept are similar in date; so, too, the 'diamond' facing of the stair turret outside and the massive columns supporting the tower within.

The narrow lancets in the chancel indicate some modest alterations in the early thirteenth century, but the story of the town from the late twelfth century is of gentle stagnation in face of the rise of neighbouring Sherborne. The alterations of the later Middle Ages are modest: the upper parts of the tower and the carved screen. At the same time the merchant guild of the town seems to have been involved in a brotherhood of St John, but perhaps little more could be afforded. And was it poverty or Protestant views which found the parish in trouble with the bishop in Queen Mary's reign for not replacing necessary books and plate for the restored Mass and the figures only recently taken down from the screen?

The town's industrial prosperity from the late seventeenth century, based on brewing, textiles and leather processing, drew in labour with but modest means. The church, no greater in size than soon after the Conquest, could only accommodate the increasing population in galleries, including one over the screen. A new north aisle with gallery made room for an extra 220 in 1826 and the average congregation in 1851 was 370. But the population of the whole parish in that year was 1746 and there was seating in church for rather fewer than half that number (although Congregationalists and Methodists were doing well). In fact in the 1840s some of the older galleries had actually been removed, presumably for structural reasons, and the north transept and part of the chancel were rebuilt. More, clearly, needed to be done, and between 1867 and 1869 the heavy hand of Henry Hall of London came down and the nave and north aisle were entirely demolished and rebuilt nearly 30 feet longer in a very undistinguished style.

These changes were, presumably, signs of life. They came under two vicars who actually lived in the parish, a vast improvement on the record of George Isaac Huntingford, vicar from 1789 until 1825. For the whole of that period he lived at Winchester College where he was warden, from 1802 until 1815 he was also bishop of Gloucester, and from 1815 bishop of Hereford instead. His curate, living in the old and dilapidated Vicarage, may well have been a better inspiration.

Later in the nineteenth century mission rooms were built in strategic parts of the parish and from 1940 the vicar of Milborne Port has been rector of Goathill, itself in Dorset. How very fitting ! Goathill might well have been part of that great minster parish a thousand and more years ago.

V.C.H. Somerset vii (forthcoming); Winchester College, *Sixth-Centenary Essays*, 351–74.

The Norman Mission
LULLINGTON, *All Saints*

~✕~

There is plenty of Norman work to be seen in Somerset but surely none so fine as in this tiny church north of Frome on the Wiltshire border. The size of the village explains the survival of the church: such a small community would have needed no more space in their church even at the time when most were being enlarged, although William Horton, a clothman and owner of a fulling mill nearby, and his brother Thomas Horton, also a clothman from Iford, could probably have afforded to pay for complete rebuilding. When he died in 1508 William left just enough for repairs; and his son in 1529 gave something to buy a mass book and vestments. Perhaps in William's time the tower was given an upper stage with two-light bell openings, battlements and a stair turret; and two square-headed windows were also inserted to give more light. Two two-light windows had already been put in a century earlier.

But that was all. The parish was evidently content, and rightly so: they had changed the shape of the arches under the central tower from the original semi-circular shape,

Lullington: *font*   **Lullington:** *north door*

Lullington: *All Saints' church from the green*

probably when the tower was raised. Nothing else was done to alter the north and south doorways and the magnificent font, the most highly decorated in Somerset. The north doorway is perhaps the most startling; it would only have been seen when the door was used for processions, and yet the sculptor put his best work in it. It consists of a tall tympanum with a tree of life, flanked by two beasts, framed by rings; and above it a seated figure, surely God the Father, under a steep gable. And all around zigzags, beak heads, scallop capitals, spirals and abaci.

The simpler south doorway leads into the other surprise, and the most eloquent state-ment of the Faith of the Church. Carved around the font are the words *Hoc Fontis Sacro Pereunt Delicta Lavacro* – in the sacred washing of the font sins are cleansed. The vigorous banded carving begins at the bottom of the bowl with interlocking arcading, then flowers, then the inscription then, at the rim, monsters and demons. Or should it be read the other way: monsters and demons lying in wait for the soul but, after baptism, the prospect of flower-strewn meadows and heavenly mansions?

When and by whom was all this done? Experts date the work to the 1130s and link it stylistically to contemporary work at Old Sarum. For much of the twelfth century the owners of Lullington were successive members of the Wasprey family: Robert, his mother Felicia (alive before 1193), her father Aldhelm and his father Geoffrey. It is probable that the Waspreys held Lullington of one of the great feudal lords of the time: Edward of Salisbury, his son Walter (died 1147) and his grandson Patrick (died 1168). This link would explain Wiltshire influence at Lullington. Whatever the truth, Lullington remains a telling example of the vigour of the Church in the century after the Conquest. In its present setting on the edge of a green in a model Victorian village, it is also a fine example of the continuity of the link between squire and church, a bond which gave the parish church its birth and remained its economic lifeblood until the present century.

Medieval Deeds of Bath and District (S.R.S. lxxiii), pp. 56–7; *Cartulary of Cirencester Abbey*, ii, pp. 516–18; J.H. Bettey, *Wessex from AD 1000*, 77–8; information from Mrs A. Crown and D. H. Brookes.

International Scholar
YATTON, *St Mary the Virgin*

~❧~

In 1066 John the Dane held a huge estate in the moors between the Mendips and the sea, but his was the wrong race and the wrong political side. William the Conqueror, dispossessing all but a few of the landowners of Edward the Confessor's time, gave John's land at Clevedon to Matthew of Mortagne and his estate at Yatton to Giso, bishop of Wells, himself already in post since 1060 but acceptable to the new regime for he, too, was a foreigner from across the Channel, a native of Lorraine.

The Yatton land was already divided, and not simply between the lord and his tenants. The bishop held by far the largest part but three smaller holdings had been given to men who were probably members of his staff or household: Fastrad held something like a quarter share, Hildebert a fifth share, and the smallest of all was attached to the church and was held by Benzelin the archdeacon. Fastrad, who also held land of the bishop in Wells and Banwell, may well have come from Lorraine with the bishop; Hildebert held land in the bishop's manor of Evercreech and also in Clevedon and near Bruton. Both were probably laymen. Benzelin, the first archdeacon in the diocese, went on to serve Giso's successor John of Tours.

John, who became bishop in 1088, removed the seat of his bishopric from Wells to Bath in 1090, almost certainly in part because the city had recently been burnt by opponents of William Rufus and the king needed a reliable figure to rule there. The move may well have suited Bishop John, for he had been trained as a doctor and the healing springs must have held great interest for him. So to Bath moved his household; and when in 1106 formal arrangements were made by means of a charter to put the finances of the monastery there on a firm footing the witnesses included, besides colleagues such as Hervey, bishop of Bangor, and Herlewin, abbot of Glastonbury, the three archdeacons and other members of the bishop's household, the last of whom to be named was Adelard son of Fastrad. This was the young man later to be known as Adelard of Bath.

The church and its estate held in 1086 by Benzelin the archdeacon was given fifty years later by Bishop Robert as part of his endowment of Wells cathedral; it became one of the prebends, one of the estates which gave its holder the title of prebendary and membership of the cathedral chapter or governing body. The prebendary of Yatton was also the rector of the parish, but successive prebendaries were often absent and appointed vicars to carry out their parochial and pastoral duties. When the first vicar was appointed is not known, but Walter, vicar in the early fourteenth century, complained to Bishop Drokensford that his salary of £8 was insufficient to keep himself and the two chaplains needed to run the parish, considering that the prebendary's income was £66 13s 4d. The

Yatton: *St Mary the Virgin's church*

bishop was entirely sympathetic and made arrangements to put the matter right.

Yatton's prebend had thus become part of the original endowment of Wells Cathedral and the income from it made a direct contribution to the building which Bishop Robert's foresight made possible. Adelard of Bath in a very different way laid foundations whose significance went far beyond his native land, certainly far beyond the parish which may have been his birthplace. The young man was sent by the bishop first as a student to Tours and then to Laon, a common enough route for a bright young man. From Laon, probably via Salerno and Greece, Adelard went to Antioch, where he experienced a violent earthquake. That was in the year 1114.

Adelard was by no means simply a touring student; he had a serious aim in view, for he brought back with him after his seven years absence a knowledge of Arabic and a number of books which proved vital to the development of science in western Europe. The books included a translation from the Arabic (Greek was not then known in the West) of Euclid's work on mathematics called *The Thirteen Elements of Euclid's Geometry* and astronomical tables called the Zij which had come from India via Baghdad. He may also have acquired the mathematical and astronomical work of Omar Khayyam. His contribution to the development of western science was thus immense.

On his return to England Adelard found a home in the king's court, where he wrote his most famous book, *Quaestiones Naturales*, an 'encyclopaedic explanation of natural phenomena' which was later translated into Hebrew. He also wrote about the ailments of falcons, and added to a well-known work on alchemy such items as how to make alcohol, how to produce sugar candy or toffee from sugar cane and how to make yellow and green dye. He was not simply a theoretical scientist; he evidently worked in the royal exchequer, which used the abacus whose use he had studied at Laon for calculating taxes and other debts to the king. He also dabbled, like most scientists at the time, in alchemy and he is known to have cast horoscopes for kings Stephen and Henry II.

None of the rectors and prebendaries of Yatton who succeeded Benzelin were as distinguished as Adelard, though many of them were graduates of English universities and among them were Thomas Purveour (prebendary from 1451), a native of Beckington and a doctor of Theology from Padua, Richard Nykke (by 1488 until 1494), also a Somerset man, who was a graduate of Oxford, Cambridge, Ferrara and Bologna and John Taylour (by 1522–34), the eldest of triplets and also educated at Ferrara. Prebendaries after the Reformation included Samuel Ward (1610–15), professor of Divinity at Cambridge and one of the translators of the Apocrypha; and George Downham (1615–16), professor of Logic at Cambridge and bishop of Derry 1617–34.

One other interest of Adelard was an instrument for measuring heights based on a triangle. Masons who built our churches were practical men, not higher mathematicians; their calculations were based on experience, but their skill allowed them to make windows larger, towers higher, arches wider and arcades more slender. Yatton church

Yatton: *prebendal house*

illustrates in its transition between Decorated and Perpendicular the great leap forward which took place in English church building between the late thirteenth and the early sixteenth century.

The progress of the rebuilding can be charted through the churchwardens' accounts which have survived from 1445. Notable are the clerestoried nave, the west front, the truncated spire and the exquisite south porch. Inside the porch the lierne vault includes a shield with a puzzling device no herald would acknowledge; outside the ogee gable above the doorway reaches to an angel bereft of his wings. Above again, in the pierced parapet which runs around aisles and clerestory, is a shield of arms which represents the families of Cheddar and Sherborne. The shield thus records the generosity of Yatton's great benefactors in the late fifteenth century, Sir John Newton and his heiress wife Isabel Cheddar. They lie, composed in death, on a fine tomb befitting such generous benefactors. The modern addition, known as the Chapter House and reflecting in its shape the truncated spire, was designed by Andrew Pittman.

J.A. Robinson, *Somerset Historical Essays*, 73; *Two Chartularies of Bath Priory* (S.R.S. vii), pp. 53–4; *Wells Cathedral Manuscripts* i. 385–6; L. Cochrane, *Adelard of Bath: the first English scientist; Churchwardens Accounts* (S.R.S. iv), 78–172; *Proc. Som. Arch. Soc.* xliv. 58–9.

COMPTON MARTIN, *St Michael*

Somerset has not produced many saints – Dunstan, of course; Stephen Harding (d. 1134), third abbot of Citeaux and born somewhere near Porlock; and Alphege, martyred archbishop of Canterbury (d. 1012), who was a hermit somewhere in the county before becoming abbot of Bath. Another in that distinguished band was Wulfric, usually known as Wulfric of Haselbury from the village near Crewkerne where he lived as a hermit from 1125 until his death in 1154.

But Wulfric was born in Compton Martin, in the heart of the Mendips and on one of the estates of a great Norman landowner, William FitzWalter. He took Holy Orders and served at Deverill in the diocese of Salisbury, spending much of his time hunting and hawking, hardly the model priest. A chance conversation with a beggar forced him to take his vocation more seriously and he returned to his native parish in the early 1120s.

Compton Martin: *interior*

Here he served until 1125, growing increasingly uneasy at the comfortable life he still led in his lord's household.

So William FitzWalter found him a cell beside the parish church on another of his estates, Haselbury Plucknett, and provided him with a shirt of chain mail to increase his mortifications. Wulfric soon discovered that the shirt was too long and made genuflecting difficult. The power of Wulfric's prayers enabled William to cut the chain mail with a pair of shears as if it were cloth. It was partly a question of faith, partly that he who shared in this kind of holy warfare by providing weapons would thereby share in the victory.

The saint would probably recognise the church at Compton. It is a remakable survival in a county whose prosperity in the fifteenth century destroyed more than Victorian restorers swept aside. Here are a Norman chancel, Norman arcades forming aisles north and south of a nave; a Norman clerestory, corbel table and font. One of the nave piers has spiral fluting, much like Durham but with a lighter touch.

There is some later work, inevitably of the later Middle Ages. The chancel arch and the last arch on the south arcade were altered when a chapel was built on the south side of the chancel. Then, too, the present nave windows were inserted and the west tower added, the latter apparently suffering from several changes of plan.

Compton Martin: *St Wulfric*

The holiness so evident in Wulfric's life was a great attraction in the twelfth century. William FitzWalter was evidently proud of him if unable quite to trust the prophet after knowing the hunting priest. There may have been some political credit, for Wulfric made no secret of his support for Stephen in the Civil War although he was quite prepared to criticise the king to his face. The unseemly attempts both by the Cistercian monks of Forde (one of whom later was the author of Wulfric's 'Life') and the Cluniacs of Montacute (who supplied him with food every day) to acquire his body indicate the financial advantage of owning holy bones.

Wulfric's physical world may have been strictly confined in his cell at Haselbury, but the world came to him including at least two kings, Henry I and Stephen, for his gifts of prophecy soon became well known and his power as a healer, too, was great. The single

Compton Martin: *St Michael's church*

window in the north-west corner of the church is all that reminds the visitor of the man who served here so long ago when the little parish of Compton was in the care of a single priest. The splendid collection of kneelers, each one recalling one of the dioceses in the country, sets this church in a wider context, just as Wulfric's cell was open to a wider world. Ever since 1981 Compton and its neighbours Ubley, Blagdon and Charterhouse have been officially joined together as a single living; and in 1993 a woman deacon was appointed to the living with the title 'deacon-in-charge'. Could St Wulfric ever have foreseen such a development ?

Wulfric of Haselbury by John, abbot of Ford (S.R.S. xlvii).

Normandy in England
STOGURSEY, *St Andrew*

From a distance the church seems to be hiding shyly at the bottom of Stogursey's main street; on closer inspection the massive tower and high roofs are still no preparation for the Romanesque magnificence within. It is undoubtedly the finest Norman church in the diocese, but why so large ? An already imposing church, its former chancel replaced by an aisled choir to serve a small monastic community, leaving a nave, transepts and crossing for the parish.

The fine Romanesque capitals of the crossing have close parallels in central and western France and that is not surprising for the Domesday lord of Stogursey was William de Falaise, who came from the birthplace of the Conqueror himself. Those eight crossing capitals and the herring-bone construction of the massive square tower both show a nice mixture of Saxon and Norman motifs which indicate a church built in the 1080s or

Stogursey: *interior, 1836*

36

1090s, no doubt with the generous support of Stogursey's lord. Excavation has revealed that the original church had apses to chancel and transepts.

At some date very early in the twelfth century another lord of Stogursey, a second William de Falaise, gave the church of the parish to the abbey of Lonlay, which lies some 30 miles south-west of Falaise. Probably about 1120 Lonlay sent over some monks to establish a religious community, but not until about 1175–80 were the original chancel and transepts extended eastwards to form an aisled choir, a fitting place for the community to worship separately from the lay parishioners. The dog tooth decoration of the arcade has close parallels not this time with France but with the more English tradition to be found at the same date at Glastonbury. The massive square pillar bases of the arcade may indicate the original floor level under which lay a crypt.

In those early days landowners continued to hold estates on both sides of the English Channel, but hard decisions had to be made after the loss of Normandy by King John. Bruton priory, for example, found it sensible to exchange their Norman estates for lands of Norman abbeys in England. Lonlay had no such intention and thus in time of war between England and France Stogursey priory as a French possession was considered to be 'alien'. Many of the priors and monks were obviously not English, and the flow of profits from the priory's estates was often interrupted during the fourteenth and early

fifteenth centuries as the Crown took over the establishment for the duration of hostilities. An inventory of goods and furnishings drawn up in 1324 during one such period of seizure mentions a hall, chamber, cellar, kitchen, bakehouse, brewhouse and barn. The rooms and their contents would describe any respectable farm of the time. There is nothing in the inventory, apart from its heading, to show that this was in any sense a monastic establishment.

The monastic community, never very large after the late twelfth century, must have suffered the consequences of uncertainty and the long distance from home. Charges of maladministration were brought against several priors and more than one monk was sent home. The Crown sometimes diverted income to secular uses and the estates were prey to the greed of local landowners. In the fifteenth century more than half the income was paid as a pension first to Queen Joan, widow of Henry IV, and later to her son

Stogursey: *bench end showing spoonbill*

Humphrey, duke of Gloucester. The community life of the priory could hardly have existed. In 1443–4 the priory was eventually closed and its land, rents and the tithes paid by parishioners passed into the hands of Eton College.

The spiritual life of the parish was not directly affected by the priory. There are no records, as at Dunster, of disputes between parish and priory and there is no record of local opposition when in 1402 Richard Amys, the prior, was appointed by the bishop to undertake the parochial duties of the vicar, William Horton, who was described by the bishop as 'wearied with so great infirmity that he does not suffice for the cure'. But Richard Vyse, the last prior, evidently made an enemy of John Verney of Fairfield, whom Vyse accused of preaching in English in church against both himself and the vicar. Verney was perhaps justified in his opposition to the prior who, having joined the monks at Bath when he left Stogursey, found it not to his taste and left.

The parish was a busy one, having in 1535 a vicar, a curate and two chaplains. Vicars were, however, often pluralists and absent and in the early sixteenth century William Wallschaw wrote to the provost of Eton lamenting:

> God knoweth the pariche of Stokegursy was never
> so owte of order as hit is now and all for lake of a
> goode hed and a sad curate and lernyd.

The church, obviously larger than the parishioners really needed, was by the early sixteenth century the focus of great care and concern. There was an active brotherhood of Our Lady which grew out of a fund to commemorate the dead, and there were altars or chapels within the great church dedicated to Our Lady and to the Holy Trinity and lights before the images of St Anne, St George, St Erasmus, Our Lady of Pity, the Trinity and the Holy Rood. The strength of the parish, as distinct from the interest of Eton College as the rectors and thus owners and repairers of the choir, is reflected in the fact that the nave was rebuilt about 1500 and furnished in the next twenty or thirty years.

A man, usually called simply 'carver' and only once as 'Glosse the carver', began work for the parish in 1524–5 and in the first year was paid £11 9s 8d which included trips to Wales and to Bristol. Quantities of timber from nearby Fiddington and local labour used to carry and saw it strongly suggests that the nave was being reroofed. The resulting panelled ceiling, the panels formed by narrow carved ribs, survived until the nineteenth century. The sale of old oak in 1824 raised the princely sum of £4 9s. Smaller sums paid in 1527–9 may have been for some of the seats, although one or two of those were made later, probably in the 1530s with money raised by the young men of the parish selling ale. The initials ES and IS may refer to Elizabeth and Isabel Symonds whose names appear in the accounts when 23s 6d was spent on seats.

Perhaps the most fascinating carved motif to be found on the bench ends is the spoonbill whose presence presumably proves that such birds lived in the Parrett estuary in the

Stogursey: *St Andrew's church*

sixteenth century as well as in the bishop of London's park at Fulham and elsewhere in East Anglia, and Sussex. It is another example of the slightly exotic in Stogursey's history; and it is not all something in the distant past and nearly forgotten. Fr Michael Lewis, a former curate of Stogursey, found in the parish church of Lonlay (actually a substantial portion of the twelfth-century abbey church) a map of her ancient dependencies, of which Stogursey was, of course, one. The discovery led eventually to the twinning of the two communities of Stogursey and Lonlay L'Abbaye in 1986 and to the gift to Lonlay of one of Stogursey's carved bench ends, which is now proudly displayed, a piece of West Country carving in the heart of the French countryside.

V.C.H. Somerset vi. 154–6; *Stogursey Charters* (S.R.S. lxi); *Churchwardens Accounts* (S.R.S. forthcoming). P. Ellson recognised the Symonds initials: *S.D.N.Q.* xxxiii. 148–9.

The Lay Brothers of Witham
WITHAM FRIARY, *St Mary,*
St John the Baptist and All Saints

~❧~

Travellers by the railway between Westbury and Taunton see a building with a high pitched roof of red tiles and a heavily-buttressed apse, for all the world like some High Victorian city sanctuary towering over its slums; or perhaps something more Continental, a massive abbey church surrounded by farmsteads in a remote Burgundian hamlet. Witham's bellcote is, of course, a sign of modesty and the surrounding village, a collection of old and new and far from slums, is small, nestling in the narrow valley of the river Frome. The great monastic historian David Knowles was attracted here as a schoolboy from Downside not by the church but by the trains, and thus it was that he could write so evocatively about the place; about the Carthusian monks who built the village church in the late twelfth century for their community of lay brethren, and about their own great cloister which was to be so rudely and misleadingly divided from its dependency by the engineering works of the Great Western Railway.

Friary comes from *frerie*, the settlement of lay brothers, that essential part of every Carthusian community, and Witham was England's oldest, founded as part of Henry II's penance for the murder of Archbishop Becket. In order that the monks might devote their entire energies to prayer and meditation largely confined to their cells around the great cloister, lay brothers under the guidance of the monastic go-between known as the procurator tilled the soil and generally ensured that their seclusion was complete. The lay brothers, living celibate lives under a modified version of the Rule, usually lived on a separate site some distance from the monks. That was the ideal of the early years. In the course of time such an ideal had to be modified: in 1318 John Fisher of Witham agreed to act as fisherman, plumber or general factotum for the prior, and in return accepted food, clothing and cash for himself and his wife.

The great cloister of the Witham Charterhouse, as each community of the Order was called after the mother house, the Grande Chartreuse above Grenoble, lies just south of the railway on a knoll above the River Frome in what was in the late twelfth century unpromising land within the forest of Selwood. Monks from the mother house arrived c. 1178–9 under the rather impractical prior Narbert and found no welcome either from the peasants whose land they had been given nor from the uncongenial drenching gales of Somerset. A second prior died soon after his arrival to replace Narbert, and it was only the personality and ability of the third prior which brought success. His name was Hugh of Avalon, a native of Burgundy, who for many years had been procurator at the Grande Chartreuse.

Witham Friary: *interior*

Hugh came to Witham probably in 1180, reluctantly, but at the instance of Henry II himself and at the persuasion of Bishop Reginald, who visited Hugh on his way home from the third Lateran Council. His first task was to build the 'upper house' for his monks in stone; his second the 'lower house', at first a series of wooden buildings arranged in a circle. This was to be the nucleus of the present village, and its first permanent building, probably the work of Hugh, was the church which later was to become Witham's parish church. Today's visitor who has also been to contemporary churches in France, will recognise in the simple rib vaulting and the deeply splayed windows in the apse a building more reminiscent of Burgundy or Provence than England's West Country.

The qualities Hugh showed as prior at Witham could not be confined to his cell and cloister. Henry II recognised his great worth and in the summer of 1186 chose him to be bishop of Lincoln, a huge see stretching from the Thames to the Humber. But late every summer until his death in 1200 Hugh returned to his cell at Witham for a month or more, back to the contemplative life he had chosen so long before and so far away. No longer prior, he still retained great influence there and his sanctity as well as his organising ability were widely known and appreciated. He was, in David Knowles's words, 'the last of a long line of sainted monk-bishops', the builder of Lincoln cathedral, a rare character who overcame outbursts of royal anger by a joke or a playful shake; a rare

Witham Friary: *exterior*

bishop who in an age of political prelates devoted his energies to his clergy and people; for Ruskin 'the most beautiful sacerdotal figure known to me in history'.

By nature the life of a Charterhouse was contemplative and withdrawn from the world, almost a light under a bushel. But the spirit of Hugh's foundation at Witham survived hardly diminished until the Dissolution in 1539. Changes there in the fifteenth century reflected the growth of the lay community across the valley from the monastery. In 1443 the diocesan bishop gave the monks permission to build a dormitory both for the use of unmarried lay brothers and for guests. The place was evidently attracting people from outside as it had done in Hugh's day. In 1459 the prior requested the bishop's permission to have a font in the lay brothers' church, thus marking the emergence of a full secular community in the hamlet.

When the great cloister on the hill was abandoned in 1539 – soon to become part of a private house – the fishponds in the valley were still full of fish and the people of the 'frerie' remained to serve the new owner of the estate. Perhaps for a time the dormitory housed farm stock or produce or was converted to dwellings. A dovecot was certainly preserved and still stands as a reminder of the monastic origin of the village. And the little church, given a tower in the eighteenth century and a replacement bellcote in the nineteenth, remained as the place of worship, no longer exclusively for lay brothers as designed by St Hugh but for the whole secular community. The massive buttresses built by William White in 1876 were the price to pay for the survival of St Hugh's simple church. It is, in Somerset, the only contemporary link with the saint who loved the place so well. But it is not the only link. The Roman Catholic church at Radstock is dedicated to him, and in 1978 the Hugh of Witham Foundation was formed in association with the ecumenical study centre at Ammerdown, in part to commemorate the man who, coming to a foreign land under obedience, managed to combine the active and the contemplative in a busy life.

M.D. Knowles, *The Monastic Order in England*, 375–91; *English Episcopal Acta: Bath and Wells, 1061–1205*, lxv; R.W. Dunning, 'The West-Country Carthusians' in *Religious Belief and Ecclesiastical Careers in Late Medieval England*, 33–42; M. McGarvie, *Witham Friary, Church and Parish*; B. Fletcher, R. Dunning [and I. Burrow], *Saint Hugh of Witham and his Priory*.

A Bishop's foundation
HUISH EPISCOPI, *St Mary*

The diocese of Bath and Wells, then known simply as Wells, was formed out of the huge see of Sherborne in 909 with Athelm, St Dunstan's uncle, as its first bishop. By the time of Edward the Confessor, one of Athelm's successors Giso of Lorraine had become a substantial landowner in Somerset, in 1065 lord of manors stretching between Banwell, Yatton and Chew Magna in the north, Wiveliscombe, Wellington and Lydeard in the west, and Combe St Nicholas, Winsham and Chard in the south. In the centre were the great manor of Wells besides Westbury and Wedmore. Combe, Winsham and Chard formed for tax purposes part of the bishop's large estate of Kingsbury, and among its other 'members' were Lytlenige, Hiwisc, Cuma and Pybbesbyrig, the first signifying an island, the second a homestead. Today the bishops' connection with some of these estates is still remembered in their names: Bishops Lydeard, Kingsbury Episcopi, Huish Episcopi.

In their concern to rebuild and endow their cathedral at Wells and provide for the administration of the diocese, successive bishops gave some of their estates including Combe, Winsham and part of Wells to the cathedral, but others remained to support the bishop's proper state and dignity. The land at Huish (as Lytlenige and Hiwisc came to be called) had in 1086 arable land for eight ploughteams, 100 acres of pasture, 12 acres of meadow and 20 acres of woodland, mostly in the south-west of the parish, and later a deer park. Much land was evidently recovered from the marshes of the Yeo and Parrett, and still in the middle of the nineteenth century there were nearly 1000 acres in church hands. The estate passed from bishop to bishop until 1548 when Bishop William Barlow was forced to surrender it to the duke of Somerset. Two years later Barlow recovered it and his succesors continued to enjoy the income from it until 1855 when it passed to the Ecclesiastical Commissioners. Most of the land was sold to the sitting tenant farmers in the next two years but the last piece did not pass out of church hands until 1952.

One part of the original estate was given away long before, namely the land and tithes of the parish church, which between 1179 and 1199 were given for the endowment of the archdeaconry of Wells. From then onwards successive archdeacons received most of the tithes of corn grown there and the rent or produce from over 70 acres of land. They also appointed vicars to serve the parish. In practice the archdeacons let their property for which the tenant in 1547 paid £28 a year. Almost incredibly the same sum was still paid by the tenant in 1897. Those tenants, in their turn, usually charged much more realistic rents to their sub-tenants. The Tucker family in 1650 received £142, a handsome profit. That profit increased as time went on: in 1799 the archdeacon's tithes were commuted for corn rents worth over £278. From 1808 the new lessee privileged to enjoy this

Huish Episcopi: *tower*

Huish Episcopi: *south doorway*

bounty was none other than Prebendary Walker King, very soon to be bishop of Rochester and already a residentiary canon of Wells and vicar of Burnham.

The present parish church to which successive archdeacons appointed vicars has a famous west tower, made more famous still in 1972 after its appearance on a postage stamp. That tower is not its first, for the church standing when it was handed over to the archdeacon had a central tower, part of whose stair survives in the thickness of the wall of the north transept. The date of the first church on the site is quite uncertain, but it is likely to have been founded by one of the pre-Conquest bishops before the creation of Langport, since Langport's church was a dependent chapelry.

The ornate south doorway is of the twelfth century and suggests by then an elaborate building designed by episcopal craftsmen. Its golden Ham stone is discoloured by fire and reference to the dedication of the church about 1232 suggests that a disaster had occurred. Subsequent work in the fourteenth and fifteenth centuries has hidden that thirteenth-century rebuilding very successfully: the chancel, the porch and probably both transepts were altered in the fourteenth century, the chancel arch, the south transept and its extension west to the porch in the fifteenth when the central tower was evidently taken down. The west tower, best seen through the blossom of the apple orchard to the west, probably dates from about 1505.

V.C.H. Somerset iii. 9–11.

46

BURNHAM ON SEA, *St Andrew*

Bishop Walter Haselshaw, bishop of Bath and Wells 1302–8, had it in mind to rearrange the finances of Burnham rectory. In 1306 he gave the patronage, the right of appointing the rector, to the chapter at Wells, but he died before doing anything further. Early in 1310 his successor John Drokensford wrote to Henry, the rector, reminding him that, like his predecessors, he was obliged to pay £10 a year towards the maintenance of the cathedral services. He also wrote to the chapter intimating that, on his expected arrival in the diocese from Rockbourne in Hampshire, he would arrange a more permanent solution from which the cathedral would benefit further.

Exactly what happened next is not known, but presumably either Drokensford or his successor Ralph of Shrewsbury arranged that the cathedral should have a greater share of the income from Burnham church, in return for which the chapter had to appoint a vicar to serve the parish. The exact arrangements were settled in 1336. Under them

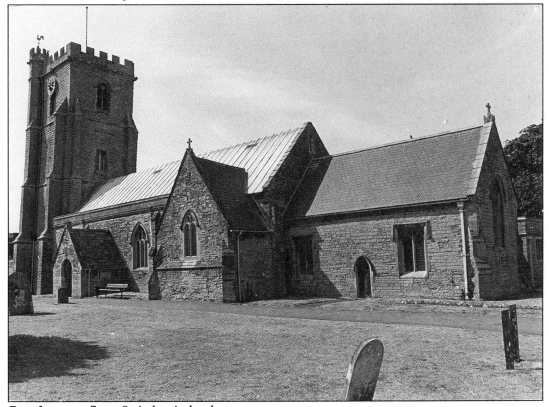

Burnham on Sea: *St Andrew's church*

Burnham on Sea: *altarpiece*

successive vicars were to have the tithes of hay, reeds, fish, mills, lambs, wool, cheese, calves, foals, flax, hemp, pigeons, pigs, honey, garden produce and fowls, and also the regular parish offerings, and the grass of the churchyard and of the yard of a dependent chapel elsewhere in the parish. The cathedral would receive a much larger sum from the tithes of sheep and corn. Out of his share the vicar had to pay a chaplain to serve the chapel and find the archdeacon's visitation fees, buy two processional candles, incense, bread and wine for communion, repair service books and have vestments washed. The cathedral had to pay for new books and vestments and cover all other costs including repairs to the chancel of the parish church and a new house for the vicar to live in. The house had still not been built in 1343–4.

Long before all these arrangements had been settled the parish church itself had been entirely built from its foundations. From York in October 1314 Bishop Drokensford sent a commission to his suffragan in the diocese, the Franciscan Gilbert O'Tigernaig, bishop of Enachdun (Annaghdown), exiled from his titular see in Ireland, requesting him to consecrate it. For some reason this was not done, and in the following summer Drokensford came in person and dedicated the new building 'in the name of Christ and to St Andrew's honour'. A year later again, in September 1316, the ceremony was made official by an entry in the bishop's register to ensure that 'the dedication feast may be devoutly kept'. And a significant phrase was added: the bishop promised forty days indulgence to visitors to the new church duly contrite and confessed, who were prepared to make an offering. The building fund was still open.

Only a small part of that new church now certainly remains, the present south transept with its cinquefoiled two-light window and the cinquefoiled recesses, although the walls of the long nave and the short chancel are probably of the same date. The rather plain tower was added later in the fourteenth century and windows and possibly the chancel arch were fifteenth-century replacements. Richard Swan, a canon of Wells and a former vicar (1449–58), left £10 for repairs to the chancel in his will of 1486, and one bench end surviving in the late eighteenth century recorded that Thomas Peter gave money for seven seats. Wills of the 1540s refer to the high altar, an altar or statue of St Nicholas, a light before the High Cross above the rood screen, and a fund in the name of the Virgin Mary. The north aisle, the last addition to the church, was built in 1838.

During the Middle Ages the cathedral carried out its responsibilities for the fabric of the chancel. Eleven account rolls surviving from between 1352 and 1538 include expenditure on the stone tiled roof in 1352, the roof and glass in 1402 and 1417, desks and benches in 1414, and glass in 1436 and 1538. The cathedral also appointed successive vicars, and over the years were obviously tempted to select one of their own number, thus increasing the income of clergymen already well provided for. Thus it was, for example, that in 1727 Robert Creyghton of Wells was nominated by his influential father and namesake, the Precentor of Wells; and thus it was – how scandalous it seems now, though not unusual then – that Dr Walker King, already holding the rich prebend of Wiveliscombe in the cathedral and living in one of the canonical houses in the city, with regular duties in the cathedral, was appointed vicar of Burnham in 1799 with no intention of moving house. Ten years later the same Dr King was consecrated bishop of Rochester and was permitted to keep his house and his two benefices. He enjoyed them all until his death in 1827.

Walker King made one contribution to his parish church which he wanted everyone to know about, and which his successors have largely failed to appreciate. His were philanthropic motives, openly declared in a pamphlet published a year before his death, in which he described how he had installed some marble carvings by Inigo Jones in the chancel. The pamphlet, entitled *An Account of the Marble Altar Piece placed in the Chancel of the Parish Church of Burnham*, was to be sold (at prices varying between 1s 6d and 5s depending on paper quality) to any stranger who should apply to the sexton for access to view. After suitable compensation for the sexton, the proceeds were to be given to charitable purposes under the direction of the parish minister with preference for the dispensaries at Wiveliscombe and Bridgwater and the Institution for Scrofulous Diseases at Weston super Mare in which the bishop took an interest.

The marble altarpiece had a curious history. Walker King and many of his contemporaries believed it to have been designed by Inigo Jones for Charles II's chapel in Whitehall palace. In that they were shown by H. Avray Tipping to have been wrong. Instead it was designed by Christopher Wren for the very different chapel in the same palace, the chapel erected by James II for the restored Roman Catholic liturgy. Its interior had been magnificent, thoroughly impressing John Evelyn on his visit at the end of December 1686 – painted ceilings by Antonio Verrio, woodwork by Grinling Gibbons and the altarpiece, Wren's concept

Burnham on Sea: *one of Grinling Gibbons's marble cherubs*

but executed by Gibbons and his assistant Arnold Quellin the younger for the sum of £1875 1s 8d. Evelyn knew nothing of Quellin's involvement and thought that Gibbons had made the statues of St John, St Peter, St Paul and the Church. Most likely Quellin carved these statues and the great angels, Gibbons the heads of the child angels.

The altarpiece survived the fire at Whitehall and by 1708 had found its way via Hampton Court to Westminster Abbey. It was considered to be no longer suitable there when preparations were being made for George IV's coronation in 1820 and the whole or part was offered to Walker King, himself a former prebendary of Westminster and the abbey's closest episcopal friend, the first bishop of Rochester for many years not also to hold the deanery of Westminster.

King brought some of the altarpiece to Burnham, having failed to find a 'convenient situation' in his own diocese. One of his successors was evidently less than enamoured of it and it was dismantled. Parts were later found among lumber by a later vicar and were restored to the church in their present puzzling arrangement. Other parts have found their way via Lowther Castle in Cumbria to Sledmere House, Humberside. Quellin's angels are on the south wall of the tower, Gibbons's cherubs, probably modelled on his own children, partly in the tower, partly under the east window. Two angels and two cruets are part of the reredos.

Proc. Som. Arch. Soc. lxxxi. 127–32; *Country Life*, 21 March 1914; *The Times*, 28 August 1995.

A Capital Church
SOMERTON, *St Michael*

᪥

For a glorious few years between 1278 and 1366 the little town of Somerton was Somerset's county town. It played host to the king's justices, kept the king's prisoners, offered hospitality to the county's leaders. Somerton prospered, its farmers' lands increased by the rich new grasslands of Kingsmoor, their products finding their way into the town's new market, laid out on the south side of the church before 1290.

During this time of prosperity the people of Somerton spent money on their church. Curiously, it had begun as a chapel, dependent until a grant by the Empress Matilda on the mother church of Queen Camel. From about 1140 it became, in its turn, a mother church with its own burial ground but in fact it was controlled by the monks of Muchelney, who usually appointed vicars and took most of the tithes.

The present building started as a cruciform structure in the earlier thirteenth century – chancel, central tower with transepts, and aisleless nave. Features of this building are the

Somerton: *view from Market Place*

transept arches, two lancet windows and a trefoil-headed piscina. Work seems to have continued sporadically; in 1278 the king gave some timber to repair the belfry, and the north window of the north transept has tracery of about 1300.

Much more radical was work about the middle of the fourteenth century when the nave was demolished and replaced by a new nave with aisles. Rare consecration crosses cut into the stonework at each end of the south arcade record the spots where the bishop paused to bless the new work with holy water. The mouldings of the arcades, the fine reticulated tracery of the windows and the flowing tracery of the great west window are typical of quality work of the period, so often in Somerset replaced in the next century. Indeed, the chancel was rebuilt in the fifteenth century and a clerestory added at the same time above the nave. And above that, about 1510, the very fine roof with richly carved timbers, tie beams and short king-posts, the whole divided into small square panels, a fine example of the carpenter's art.

By this time the glory of the town had long departed. The community, which in the fourteenth century had its own seal depicting the Archangel Michael, boasted only a few tradesmen but at least a thriving market in the fifteenth century. Two centuries later something of a revival took place: there were several inns around the market place, prosperous men trading in woollen cloth, linen and silk, and a parish house often let to companies of musicians and travelling players. The pulpit (1615), the communion table (1626) and the font cover are evidence of continued interest in the church.

Somerton: *pulpit, 1615*

Somerton: *chapel under the tower*

The fine series of churchwardens' accounts also records the concern for the liturgy. Somerton acquired an organ, first mentioned in the year 1636–7 and reference to organ stairs and a loft shows it was placed on the chancel screen. To find an organist the wardens first sent to Pilton for William Brooke and then to Chard for young William Soper. Soper played for six months for £2 10s; Brooke was given food and drink only. In 1638–9 the wardens paid a Mr Hamlyn for some work and two years later a Mr Hayward of Bath was paid for tuning the organ and William Squier 'for amending the draughts'.

Soon the advent of Calvinist attitudes meant the end of music in church. John Haukings bought the organ case in 1653–4 and the instrument is not mentioned again although a seat was described in 1689 as under the place where the organ had stood. Someone had a long memory. After that a century passed before music is mentioned again in the accounts. By 1787–8 the church, like many another, had a band usually known as the choir.

Over the next thirty years and more services were accompanied by the strains of bass viol, violoncello, bassoon and clarinet and the voices of a group of singers. The bass viol seems to have been put to secular uses when Thomas Baltezar, who played it in the choir, joined the band of the Corps of Volunteer Infantry raised to defend the land against Napoleon. When peace was proclaimed the churchwardens in 1805 demanded that Thomas and the viol should return. With them came James Barrett and William Lake and their clarinets, a gift from the disbanded Volunteers, accompanied by 12 new books of music purchased by subscription.

V.C.H. Somerset, iii. 129–53.

Parson and Lord
YEOVIL, *St John the Baptist*

There was a church here by the middle of the tenth century, for the will of Wynflaed directs that a payment called soul-gift should be made from two estates, from Charlton Horethorne to Milborne Port and from Chinnock to Yeovil. This is a clue that Yeovil's church might have been a minster and Brian and Moira Gittos have come to a similar conclusion on different grounds. Another clue, once among the archives of Syon abbey and now in the Public Record Office in London, is rather more significant. It is a statement by a group of clergy and laymen about the rights of the parson of Yeovil drawn up in 1219, the first of a great number of disputes which came to a crisis but not an end with the temporary imprisonment of the bishop and his household in 1349.

The dispute of 1219 was between Walerand, the rector of Yeovil, and Sir John Mautravers, patron of the living, and was heard by Bishop Jocelin of Wells and John of Bayeux in the presence of the king's justices. The clerical and lay jurors told how a property known as the 'free tenement of Yeovil' was given to St John's church by 'the

Yeovil: *St John's church*

daughter of a certain king', almost certainly the Empress Matilda, probably in the 1140s. The clerical members of the jury were Robert, the dean of Chinnock (that is Robert, priest of Chinnock, rural dean), Robert the chaplain of Brympton, Henry the chaplain of Chilton (Cantelo), Adelalm the chaplain of Mudford, and Richard the clerk of Tintinhull. These were men who knew about Yeovil's church in some detail, for they were, or their churches had been, part of it; not just neighbours but men, three significantly described as chaplains because they served dependent chapels, who still operated within what remained of Yeovil's minster parish. Later disputes, which included the dependent chapels of Kingston, Preston and Barwick and a pension payable from Sock Dennis, draw the bounds of the ancient parish still wider.

The 1219 hearing was presumably designed to settle relations between the free tenement, the grant of which had been so complicated and so full of potential problems of jurisdiction between the parson, the lord of the town, and the inhabitants. It settled nothing. There was trouble again in 1305–6 between the then parson, Robert de la More, and the people, who had to promise before the king's judges and others that when they had chosen their provost, their civic leader, for the year, he should go to the parson for approval and should swear to deliver up to him all rents and other rights which were his due. This, too, was not the end. In 1317 the parson's archives went missing and the bishop threatened to excommunicate those who had stolen them. The same problem was probably at the heart of the 1349 crisis.

In 1328 John of Rissington was instituted rector at the presentation of John Mautravers. Early in the following year he was licensed to be absent from his parish for a year, a licence granted at the suggestion of Mautravers. Later in the same year he was given a further two years absence in order to study. Such licences were quite common and the parish did not suffer for as early as the 1270s a vicar had actually served the parish. The Bishop William who was later remembered as having first arranged a decent living for the vicar was probably Bishop William Button II (1267–74).

John of Rissington was habitually absent from his parish because he was a regular member of Bishop Ralph of Shrewsbury's household and council. He was thus present when Bishop Ralph came to Yeovil on a formal visitation, a time when both clergy and parishioners were perhaps a little edgy lest their misdemeanours might be reported to their Father-in-God. The story of that visitation has been told many times from the official record entered in the bishop's register.

His Lordship arrived in some state on the Sunday next before the feast of St Martin, 8 November 1349, at the end of a year and more of terror at the devastation of the Black Death during which perhaps three vicars of the parish had died. While the bishop sang Vespers in church in the late afternoon a group of townsmen attacked and wounded some of his servants outside and then shut the bishop and others inside until after dark. They then removed them to the rectory house and held them there until rescue arrived the next morning.

The bishop's immediate reaction was to excommunicate all who had banded together against him and to lay the town and surrounding villages under interdict, thus denying the inhabitants all sacraments. Within a fortnight the apparent ringleader Roger Warmwell was brought to court in Taunton and sentenced to a huge fine of £20, public penance in Yeovil, Wells, Bath, Bristol and Somerton, and was required to go on pilgrimage to the shrine of St Thomas at Canterbury. A day or so later two other men appeared before the same judges at Bishops Lydeard. The whole diocese was to be in no doubt of the affront to the bishop's dignity; did the bishop see himself almost as another martyr?

As the excitement died down the bishop had second thoughts about the interdict and early in December suspended it until Epiphany so that the Christmas feast might be celebrated. The bloodshed in the churchyard was not so easily overcome; by law in such circumstances any corpses should be carried for burial either to Wells or Bath. Such a judgment was harsh to those not involved in the affray, so the bishop permitted funerals of Yeovil folk at Mudford or Thorne. On the same day a letter was written to Yeovil's vicar about 19 parishioners whom the bishop was prepared to forgive on condition that they performed penance in church and appeared for public fustigations on the three days of the next market. However, for some unexplained reason the letter was not sent. Instead, just before Epiphany the interdict was again suspended for a further fortnight.

There is no record of any further suspension nor its proclamation. The threat had probably been enough to produce the names of more people involved on that fateful evening. So, early in February what seems to be a final list of 57 people was drawn up, several of them glovers and tanners, and their formal appearance as penitents in church and their public beatings on the three days of the market was ordered. Two more offenders were ordered to appear in court at Wiveliscombe. Those so undergoing punishments were also to present themselves before the dean of Wells. But is it quite accidental that between the two entries in the bishop's register dealing with the offenders there should be a licence for the rector to let his church to farm for three years ? Was this a way of removing the root cause of the problem with some sort of dignity ?

Rissington finally left Yeovil in 1362 by exchanging his rectory for that of Merriott with Robert Samborne, a man already well known in the town and founder of the rich chantry of the Holy Trinity. He had for some time been acting as a kind of business manager for Rissington and in 1358 had arranged that John Pryke and Thomas de Berdestaple should act as receivers of the parson's income, the huge sum of £86 13s 4d a year. Samborne had been rector of Kingstone near Ilminster from 1349 to 1353, and in the year he came to Yeovil as rector he also became one of the rectors of Crewkerne. By 1366 he was a canon of Wells and came to be close enough to Bishop Ralph to be appointed one of his executors.

Samborne's new position changed nothing in the minds of the people of Yeovil. Another dispute erupted in 1366 which involved several burgesses including John Pryke although

Tomb of Bishop Ralph of Shrewsbury in Wells Cathedral

the old rebel Roger Warmwell was content simply to be a witness to the settlement. The documents which followed the quarrel repeated almost ad nauseam that Samborne was both parson and lord of the town. Only when the last rector was replaced at the beginning of the fifteenth century by the distant and perhaps less grasping abbess and convent of Syon was there an end. Samborne must be remembered, however, not for his local unpopularity but for his great benefaction, nothing less than a complete and splendid new church.

In his will dated and proved in 1382 Robert Samborne left most of his goods 'to be expended by my executors in the work of the church of Jevele begun by me, until it be finished', phrases which have been assumed to mean that he was responsible for the whole church. That it was built in one campaign between c. 1380 and c. 1400 is not in doubt, and that the overall design was the work of one hand, probably the master mason William Wynford, has long been accepted. A local mason, Alexander Tyneham, who held the office of provost of Yeovil, may well have been directly involved. But no rector was legally responsible for more than the fabric of the chancel, as was later agreed between Yeovil's vicar and the abbess of Syon, and why should an affluent community like this one not pay for the nave and the tower?

Yeovil: *medieval lectern*

The present building, an aisled nave and quire forming a parallelogram, with a sanctuary beyond the choir, north and south transeptal chapels, south porch and west tower was in a real sense purpose built for a liturgy which by now required a combination of open space and privacy, room enough for people to mingle while Mass was being said or sung beyond the rood screen, and room too for processsions; and at the same time space for chapels to be formed either by the building itself or by the erection of parclose screens which different social groups within a parish regarded as their particular focus for devotion. So, by the 1380s Yeovil had two chantry foundations, one served by an archpriest and two assistants, and by the time the church was finished there were, besides the vicar, several chaplains, clerks and boy scholars who served as choristers.

Wynford or another planned well, for by the middle of the fifteenth century the chantry of the Trinity in the south quire aisle and of Our Lady in the south transept had been joined by the Holy Cross chantry in the north transept and later in the century by the Name of Jesus altar in the Jesus aisle on the north side of the quire. The church was the home of a community of priests, in 1450 comprising the vicar, a chantry priest, a stipendiary priest and four anniversary priests. Four priests were still in post in 1548 besides the vicar when the end of the chantries was at hand. Perhaps the most graphic reminder of that community, apart from the shell of the building, is the fine brass reading desk, probably from East Anglia and associated with Brother Martin Forester, whose name and faceless trunk are engraved on one side. It was originally placed in the quire, surrounded by the stalls of the clergy and occupying a focal point in the liturgy. It survived the Reformation changes because the Bible it carried was essential to the reformers.

Proc. Som. Arch. Soc. xliv. 1–12; P.R.O. E 315/33/147, 179; E 326/6338–40, 6502, 8854, 9399, 12559; J.H. Harvey, *English Medieval Architects*; B. and M. Gittos, 'The Evidence for the Saxon Minster at Yeovil', *Chronicle*, 4, no 4, 95–104.

Soaring Angels
WESTONZOYLAND,
St Mary the Virgin

~✗~

The tall tower of St Mary's can be seen for miles across the flat grasslands of Sedgemoor. The modern sign of the nearby inn was repainted in 1985 to recall the stirring events which for some days three hundred years earlier saw the church become a temporary prison for men who had fought for liberty and the duke of Monmouth. The tower, and the nave roof which surprises and amazes so many as they open the door for the first time, speak of prosperity in the late fifteenth century when most of the church was built, a prosperity based on the exploitation of the surrounding grasslands.

The element 'zoy' comes from two words: Sow or Sowe, the ancient British name for a river, now disappeared, and the Saxon 'eg' or island. The first word is like the Gaulish word to do with flowing or liquid, and like the Old English and Welsh words for juice and the Irish word for milk. Water in these parts played, and still plays, a vital role in the formation of the landscape and the green-ness of the grass.

So here was an island, by the early eighth century owned by Glastonbury abbey and formed of rich, sandy loam surrounded by peat marsh. By careful drainage and land management in the first half of the thirteenth century it became one of the abbey's richest estates. Middlezoy, on the highest part of the island, was evidently the first settlement, and as the reclaimed land grew in area a second village grew up at the western end, Westonzoyland. (Othery, on the further side of Middlezoy, was the 'other' village.)

The new village of Weston must have included a church, or rather a chapel dependent on Middlezoy until some date between 1291 and 1302 when it became a separate parish church in its own right. Thirty years later, in 1332, the abbot of Glastonbury acquired a royal charter allowing a market to be held every Tuesday at Weston and also a three-day fair at the end of August. The only recognisable feature of the present church to date from that period is the effigy of the priest in the north transept.

Most of the church dates from nearly two centuries later and the initials R. B. to be found at the end of a pew, on a buttress of the south transept and in some glass in the chancel, point to the active involvement of Richard Bere, abbot of Glastonbury 1493–1524. John Selwood, Bere's predecessor as abbot, came to Weston at least once, for it was recorded that while he and Sir Reginald Stourton were walking in the village street, at some date between 1470 and 1489, Stourton fell down dead. He was, of course, just the kind of man the abbot of Glastonbury would consort with, a son of the first Baron Stourton and a

Westonzoyland: *tower*

man of political prominence who served as sheriff of the county in 1468–9. Stourton perhaps owed his office to his sympathy for the views of the earl of Warwick (the Kingmaker), and he was arrested after Warwick's flight to France in 1470. Abbot Selwood was a man to whom politicians of both parties looked for support.

The church is more popularly known for its use as a prison immediately after the battle of Sedgemoor in 1685. Adam Wheeler, a drummer in Colonel Wyndham's regiment of Wiltshire militia, recorded a total of 284 men, some of them wounded and most stripped of any clothing worth taking, brought there for safe keeping. Richard Alford, one of the churchwardens, noted in the parish register that a total of about 500 were driven there of whom 79 were wounded. Five died of their wounds on the first night and one, Francis Scott, somehow managed to get out of the north door while the watch was asleep. Next day, and probably for several days afterwards, the villagers were engaged in burying the dead found on the battlefield and were said to have reported to the vicar and church-wardens that the total number of corpses was as many as 1384. Cleaning and fumigating the church after the prisoners were removed cost the parish more than 16s. A year later Ben Page, John Keyser, Thomas Cole, James Somers and John Tugbeard earned 5s. for welcoming James II when he came to inspect the battlefield.

In the fifteenth century three distinguished men were vicars of Weston, though so distin-

Westonzoyland: *nave roof*

guished that they probably never came to the parish. Henry Abingdon, vicar 1403–36, was a delegate to two great Councils, at Constance (1415) and Basle (1432–5) which sought to bring unity to a divided Church; Richard Trappe, vicar 1486–1500, spent most of his career in Rome; and Hugh Inge, vicar from 1508, went on to become in turn bishop of Meath and archbishop of Dublin. Thomas Holt, vicar from 1639 until 1666, was deprived of his living for his Royalist opinions between 1643 and 1660. Very likely he was responsible for the practice of having two Easter communion services, one on Easter Day for the respectable folk, the other on the following Sunday for the rest.

In the 1930s the parlous state of the church roof was the subject of a national appeal and the beauty of the building came to be appreciated by a wider public. W.D. Caroe restored the roof, preserving for posterity one of the finest in the diocese. Each tie beam, supported by angel busts, carries a

Westonzoyland: *buttress with initials of Abbot Bere*

kingpost and fine tracery, and seems to be supported at its centre by a flying angel. Between each tie beam is a sub-principal, also with angels at the wallplate and with a kind of pendant reaching down from the apex. Caroe also designed the roodloft which was added above the original screen.

Visitors to the church in the 1980s, looking for traces of the battle of Sedgemoor as its third centenary came close, found both in the quality of its furnishings and in the north chapel set aside for regular prayer for peace, especially in Northern Ireland, a deep sense of the spiritual in a building that had seen a greater share of intolerance than most.

S.D.N.Q. xviii. 129; W.M. Wigfield, *The Monmouth Rebellion*, 72–3; R. Dunning, *The Monmouth Rebellion*, 75.

Object of Civic Pride
BRIDGWATER, *St Mary the Virgin*

In the third quarter of the thirteenth century the leading burgesses of Bridgwater agreed formally among themselves how they would govern their newly founded town. Among their concerns was that those who were to achieve the high office of steward of the gild of merchants would already have been stewards of the Lady Chapel or stewards of the Holy Cross, both important roles in the administration of the parish church.

The parish church was thus by that time a building with at least two chapels, and the stiff-leaf capitals at the north porch doorway imply that there was already a north aisle, built in the early thirteenth century, an entirely reasonable size for the only church of a growing town.

It was on this church that for the next three centuries the townsmen and women of Bridgwater lavished their care and devotion. John de Mulle, for instance, died in 1310 leaving cash to each of the clergymen serving there and gave the rents from two of his houses in the town to provide a taper on the Lady Chapel altar for ever. In 1348 William Maiselin left a house outside the west gate to the wardens of the lights in the chantry of Our Lady in the chancel, and to the fabric fund his best brass jug. Several other people, significantly just at the time of the Black Death, left rents or houses to one or other of the chantries.

A collection made in the parish, added to gifts from outside, raised most of the money needed for a new bell in 1318 or 1319. Even more came that way in 1366–7 when work was undertaken on the church tower – £118 7s 9 ¹/₂d from the borough, £18 14s 6d from North Bower, Haygrove, Hamp, Dunwear, Horsey and Chilton. No doubt even more came in similar fashion when the spire was built a few years later.

Through bequests, collections and outright gifts the people of the town and parish cared for the fabric of their church and paid for the maintenance of its services. By 1383 there were four chaplains and three clerks as well as the vicar, all engaged in singing or serving Masses, and by 1450 both a vicar and a deputy, a chantry priest and seven chaplains serving separate altars. The period between those two years was a time of great activity: the chantry of the Blessed Virgin in the chancel was reconstructed, the chapels of Holy Trinity and St Anne were built beside St Catherine's chapel in the north transept to replace the All Saints altar, and the Holy Cross chapel was rebuilt. Across the east end of the nave was erected a huge rood screen (parts of which still survive). The nave was rebuilt in two stages in the 1420s and the 1440s, and by the end of the fifteenth century there was a chapel of St George in the north aisle.

Only the chancel was an 'outside' responsibility, for since about 1214 St John's hospital, at the end of Eastover, had been both rector and patron, and a carved boss in the chancel ceiling with the initials W.C. suggests that the roof was restored by William Cammel, master of the hospital between 1385 and 1416. For the rest of the work in the church there still survive a remarkable number of accounts of the separate chantries and of the church as a whole, each of which begins with the names of the men who administered the funds, the same men whose names occur as office holders and craftsmen in the borough and merchants in the port.

It was therefore entirely natural that the mayor, bailiffs and burgesses, corporate Bridgwater, should have taken over church affairs and church property after the dissolution of the chantries and St John's hospital. In 1553 the corporation acquired from the Crown some of the former chantry property in the town, and in the 1560s bought the lease (and much later became sole owners) of the rectory, receiving the tithes in place of the hospital and in return paying the salaries of two priests and a schoolmaster. From 1571 they paid £20 to a minister to 'preach and teach', £13 6s 8d for a curate. The sum varied from time to time, but since the corporation paid, the corporation called the tune.

Members of that corporation, by definition and law members of the Church of England,

Bridgwater: *St Mary's church corporation pew, about 1620*

Bridgwater: *St Mary's church north choir screen*

were so very obviously in charge when about 1620 the bank of carved seats now modestly placed in the south transept was originally placed in front of the old screen. There mayor, aldermen and burgesses sat each Sunday, proud of their civic dignity; so proud, indeed, that in April 1725 they complained to the archdeacon that the vicar was ill mannered in 'beginning of prayers last Sunday morning before the Mayor and Corporation came to the church contrary to the ancient custom'. They even went so far as to refuse to pay him tithes for six months to show their displeasure.

In 1743 it was decided to repair what was known as the Corporation Aisle and to provide 24 handsome folio Common Prayer books embossed with the town's coat of arms, and from 1775 a man was paid to take care of the books and cushions there. And whether it was suitable or not, when Anne Poulett, the town's M.P., presented the corporation with a huge painting recovered from a Spanish ship also in 1775 they gave orders that it should hang above the altar.

In view of this civic control, it is understandable that relations between town and the church authorities were not always amicable. In 1720 the corporation asked the bishop whether the curate, evidently very much their man, might be promoted to the vicarage, but the bishop refused. A century later, when the bishop suggested that an extra service might be held on Sunday afternoons, the corporation declined to agree. In 1826, however, they at least realised that the church fabric needed attention and gave orders that their share, the chancel, should be stuccoed, though they were less enthusiastic about replacing the battlements outside.

The rest of the church was the responsibility of the parish and by 1844 the wardens had produced no accounts for years and the fabric needed serious attention. The parish vestry were, it seems, more concerned with more secular matters such as highways although in 1844 they did ask the mayor to provide a policeman to patrol the church-yard during services.

In 1849 action began to be taken, first by the removal of the west galleries and then through a competition among architects, won by the firm of Dickson and Brakspear of Manchester, for the complete restoration of the church. Mr Brakspear did not much care for what he found at Bridgwater; the Perpendicular style in which most of the church had been built during those great periods of activity in the late Middle Ages was not to his taste. Instead he substituted details of the Decorated period wherever he could, much to the fury of local and national antiquarians.

Beautiful drawings for the whole restoration survive to show Brakspear's meticulous attention to detail, involving the whole of the roof of nave, transepts and aisles, the tracery of the windows and the unique (and none too comfortable) pews. Only the unsuitability of the soil prevented the architect from replacing the tower and spire. In his favour was his removal of the corporation pew to the south transept.

Restorations are never permanent, and in 1992–3 the well-known spire and tower were encased in scaffolding again. Quite rightly the parish appealed to the town, and spon-sored bell-ringing and a wide variety of other money-raising efforts brought the church and its place in the town to the attention of a wider community. There still remains an odd connection between Sedgemoor District Council (successor to the old corporaion) and the vicar of Bridgwater. Each year the Council pays him £10 in respect of the tithes of Horsey, which the corporation acquired in the sixteenth century, and £33.34p for an endowed lecture which they believe to be a charity on behalf of 'wayward ladies' but which in fact is the endowment of the preacher and the schoolmaster agreed under the grant of 1571.

V.C.H. Somerset vi. 230–34; R. Dunning, *Bridgwater, History and Guide.*

Disputed Possession
DUNSTER, *St George*

~✦~

William de Mohun (I) came with the Conqueror. He came from Moyon, a little village on the road south from St Lo to Tessy in western Normandy but he had other possessions further east as far as the river Orne north of Caen. Clearly a trusted follower of Duke William, he was given estates in West Somerset from which he was charged to defend the coast from possible invasion. He built his castle on the hill by the little River Avill; the settlement beneath the hill had long been named Dunster after it.

Towards the end of his life, between 1090 and 1100, he issued a charter by which he gave the church at Dunster and tithes from neighbouring estates to the Benedictine monks of Bath. 'Pricked by the fear of God' was his declared reason for the generous gift, and like many such gifts there was much in it to do with the safety of his soul. Why a Norman should have been so generous to the Benedictines of Bath rather than to monks in his native land is a question which has no clear answer, but he may well have been

Dunster: *chancel screen*

influenced by John of Tours, another foreigner, who had recently removed his cathedral from Wells to Bath and was thus the titular abbot.

The change of ownership brought with it a change of status, for a small community of monks moved to Dunster. Exactly when they came is not known, but they were there by 1177 in buildings on the north side of the parish church. By that time, too, the church itself had been rebuilt, and from then survive the north wall of the nave and part of the west wall with its round-arched doorway.

The few monks lived in community according to their Order and the pastoral work of the parish was carried out by a vicar, a secular priest appointed by the prior of Bath. He and his servant lived in the monastic enclosure and he kept his horse in the monks' stable.

At some time during the first seventy years of the thirteenth century the chancel of the church, that part used by the monks, was rebuilt, and somewhere in the building was a chapel of St Lawrence and an altar of the Holy Rood, the latter in the loft on the western face of the central tower. A century later, when the monks numbered five, there is mention of a Lady Chapel, and the great piers which support the tower seem to mark the beginning of a grand scheme to create a cruciform church. That this was not completed may have something to do with rivalry between the monks and the parishioners about the use of the building and the timing of services, a rivalry which continued for more than a century and has left traces in the present church.

The first outbreak of hostilities is revealed in the terms of an agreement drawn up in 1357 in the presence of Sir John de Mohun, descendant of the founder and lord of Dunster, between Richard of Childeston, prior of Dunster, and his monks on the one side and the parishioners on the other. It was a question of who was in charge, who took precedence in the liturgy. The building was one church shared between two communities, but the monks evidently regarded the eastern part, probably including the crossing under the tower, as their own. Their Sunday and festival High Masses, it was agreed, should begin first and the celebrant should sprinkle holy water throughout the building if the vicar was not ready to serve in the nave. Vicar and monks should then join for a single procession before Mass at St George's altar. All this seems to suggest that there had on occasions been rival processions and unseemly behaviour.

The agreement went on to define who should provide candles at particular festivals, and indicated that parishioners had access to the whole of the building, for their candles were to be placed on St George's altar at Vespers, Mattins, High Mass and Second Vespers and they were to share in the provision of the hearse lights (? on the Rood) and the Paschal candle in the sanctuary. The prior also undertook to maintain specific parts of the building over which there had evidently been problems, namely the unfinished tower, the Lady Chapel on the north of the choir, and the north transept known as the dorter aisle, from which stairs led to the monks' dormitory. The parishioners undertook

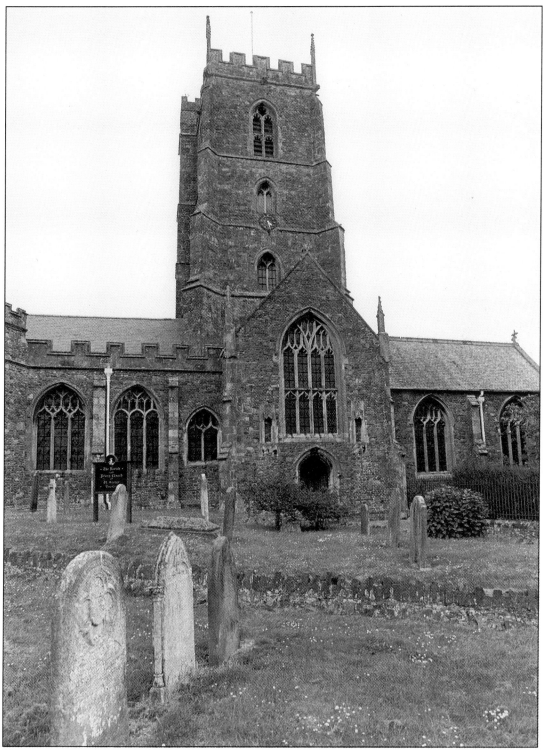

Dunster: *tower*

the care of the south transept and the south choir aisle, forming chapels dedicated to St Leonard and St Lawrence in addition to the nave, over which there was no dispute. Their main altar was in front of the south-western pier of the central tower under the rood loft which was rebuilt about 1420 thanks partly to a bequest from William Pynsoun.

Within the next century much of the structure had been rebuilt. The rather squat tower was raised one stage about 1420 and finished under a contract drawn up in 1443 between the parish and John Marys, a mason from Stogursey, according to designs by Richard Pope. The monks, this contract implies, had given up all claim to the tower; the parishioners were in a position to pay, the monks were not. The parishioners also increased the size of their nave by pulling down the south wall and creating a south aisle. The monks for their part rebuilt the choir, the Lady Chapel and the chapel of St Lawrence.

The new, wider nave created space for new chapels. A will of 1477 mentions altars of Holy Trinity, St James (the parish altar, against the south-western pier of the tower), Holy Rood, St Leonard and St Lawrence as well as the Lady Chapel, and under that same will a chantry was founded at the Trinity altar. The priest of this chantry thus joined the chantry priest of St Lawrence altar and the parish vicar in the 'choir' of the parochial part of the church.

Some years later a complaint was made in Star Chamber by the prior of Bath because the parishioners, having physically confined the monks to the eastern part of the church and demonstrated their financial independence by their building works and endowments, resented having to pay ancient dues for burials, had withdrawn wedding and burial fees, and had taken up the bell ropes so that the monks could not ring the bells. The outcome of the complaint is not known, but the quarrel evidently widened and was brought to an end by a formal agreement drawn up in 1498 whose practical terms recognised the independence of the parish and their vicar and created within the nave a parish church complete with choir, which was to be formed in front of the altar of St James. Still, on thirteen important festivals during the year parishioners were to join the monks in procession, but at other times they worshipped on their own without interference. The physical reminder of the 1498 agreement still dominates the church, the great screen which is such a splendid feature.

That was not the end of building. In 1504 a parishioner left ten tons of iron for a new aisle 'to be built or repaired on the north side', almost certainly repaired rather than newly built. And it was not the end of bickering. Some time between 1533 and 1538 the churchwardens complained to the Lord Chancellor about the state of the old rood loft against the western face of the tower. A chantry had been founded there in the later thirteenth century, the churchwardens submitted, and for two hundred years Mass had been said daily after Mattins until thirty years ago when the rood loft had come to 'extreme ruin and decay' because of the negligence of the prior of Dunster. The churchwardens now demanded that the prior of Bath should fulfil his part of the bargain because they

Dunster: *dovecot*

themselves had rebuilt the loft. In fact, of course, what they had done was to build a new screen and loft in accordance with the 1498 agreement and created a small chapel and altar in the loft beneath the Rood. The prior of Bath denied the parishioners' claim (though his own records would have proved they were correct) as well he might. It was a different loft !

Very soon afterwards there was no prior of Bath and no prior of Dunster to make claims against. In 1539 both houses of monks were dissolved and the parishioners of Dunster had to face the responsibilities of independence. The whole building was theirs. Today's parishioners, with the help of thousands of visitors, manage with a great effort to maintain their inheritance, an inheritance which their predecessors fought unusually hard to achieve.

Two Chartularies of Bath Priory (S.R.S. vii); H.C. Maxwell Lyte, *History of Dunster; S.D.N.Q.* xix. 17–20; ibid. xxii. 8–10; L.F. Salzman, *Building in England down to 1540,* 514–15.

The Faith of the People
TINTINHULL, *St Margaret*

The building is a rarity in the West of England, common enough in the east: in origin an early thirteenth-century church undivided by a chancel arch. The obvious clues are the roll-moulded string course around the inside of the building and the common width of chancel and nave. Where the design came from is an unanswerable question but surely not unconnected with the fact that the church belonged to the priory of Montacute and Montacute in its turn was part of the international family of Cluny.

The original building was lit by deep-splayed lancets with fine shafted rere-arches like the one remaining between tower and nave; that itself is a clue to the slightly later date of the tower. In the fourteenth century the church was remodelled: the present chancel arch was inserted to emphasise the distinction between nave and chancel, between worshippers and those who led worship, and tracery was added to the lancets. A century on and the lancets were replaced in the nave by much larger windows, that on the north

Tintinhull: *interior*

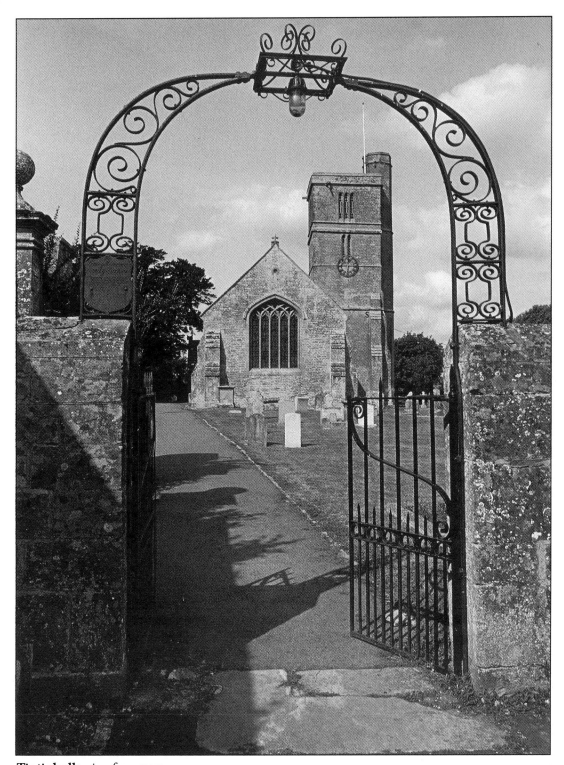

Tintinhull: *view from green*

side incorporating a light bracket. During the same period the south porch was rebuilt with a fine stone vault in 1441–2 and ten years later a stone screen and loft replaced an earlier screen. At the beginning of the sixteenth century the top stage of the tower and a stair turret were added and the carved benches were made.

All this activity is recorded in the accounts of churchwardens dating from 1433 which tell how money was raised to maintain both the services and the fabric by the traditional means of brewing ale, baking bread (from 1497 concentrated in a church house), by gifts in cash or kind from devout parishioners, and by leasing small parcels of land. John Stone, rector of the parish until his death in 1416, was a generous benefactor to a dozen or so parishioners as well as to the church and the parish brotherhood. Most of his parishioners were of more modest means, but they bought candles, bread and ale, lent a cow or a bull for a year and at their deaths left small sums in cash or whatever else came to hand which others might buy or hire for church funds – a bundle of wool, a basket of wheat or barley, a swarm of bees, a brass pot, a gown or a kerchief.

But does all this indicate genuine popular devotion or conventional concern for life insurance? Were the copper gilt cross or the silver chalice bought in 1437–8, the altar of St Nicholas, the statue of the Virgin, the painted image of a king simply outward and visible show or are they signs of spirituality? Can anything be deduced from the pastors of the parish, the succession of rectors (from 1529 vicars) in whose hands the bishop entrusted the souls of the people ?

John Hethe, rector when the churchwardens' accounts begin until his death in 1464, had been given two years study leave in 1435, until 1451 was rector of Minterne in Dorset at the same time, and from 1451 until 1464 was also rector of Chiselborough. (In 1459 he lost part of his right forefinger by accident but was permitted to continue to say Mass). Hethe's successor for two years was Robert Newton, first a Benedictine monk at Glastonbury, and from 1458 to 1461 prior of the Cluniac house of Montacute; after leaving Tintinhull he died in Rome. John Cloos (1474–7) was a scholar who almost certainly spent those years at university gaining his doctorate in theology, thus using his income from Tintinhull as a student grant. From June 1480 until April 1481 the rectory was held by John Hornse, bishop of Ross in Ireland and suffragan in Bath and Wells diocese. He was a Cistercian monk who had recently been working in London and soon after resigning Tintinhull he went back home to the north of England.

For the next thirty years the living was held in succession by John Stevens (1481-1500) and John Wyche (1501–21), the latter a lawyer perhaps employed at Wells. And then came the parish's last 'famous' parish priest, perhaps the most remarkable and certainly the best known. He was Thomas Chard who at the time he became rector was already prior of Montacute and thus patron of the living. As he could not legally present himself it was arranged that the abbot of Glastonbury should do so.

Chard could be no more than nominal rector (from 1529 he was vicar when the monks

Tintinhull: *benches with extra seat*

were permitted to appropriate most of the living). Apart from being prior he was also a bishop, one whose see was *in partibus infidelium,* in this case Selymbria in Thrace in the Ottoman Empire. The title allowed him to act as suffragan in the dioceses of Bath and Wells and Exeter.

Chard remained prior of Montacute until 1532 when he retired to the less onerous post of prior of Carswell in Devon. He may well have retired from Tintinhull at the same time. He lost his permanent home at Montacute at the Dissolution in 1539 and at the time of his death in 1541 he was living in Taunton, probably in the parish of St Mary Magdalene. In his will he gave to St Mary's a damask cope and small sums of money. In the year or two before he died he remembered Tintinhull and gave to the churchwardens a pair of vestments and some money for the bell fund.

Were such gifts in recompense for years of absence? A reading of the churchwardens' accounts of the parish while many of these absentee clergy were in office tells only of parochial devotion. Very occasionally, too, the names of the real pastors of the parish are mentioned: John the chaplain in 1433–4, Thomas Brytell or Bryten from 1434–5 to 1450 or later, Richard Walsh in 1468. These and men like them were the real spiritual leaders of many parishes, often poorly paid, unsung, even unnamed, but men who ensured that the Faith prospered.

V.C.H. Somerset iii. 262–5; *Churchwardens Accounts* (S.R.S. iv), 173–207.

A Community Church
CROSCOMBE, *Blessed Virgin Mary*

~✦~

Medieval churchwardens' accounts survive better in Bath and Wells diocese than in any other, but one such book of accounts, still in existence in 1890, is not now to be found. Fortunately, some parts of the book were then printed, and it is possible to see how the parishioners of Croscombe supported their church in the sixty years before the Reformation. Many and varied were the ways in which money was extracted from people in other parishes: at Bridgwater by rate; at Glastonbury by voluntary contributions; in Oxford by levying a toll across a busy street once a year; in most places by selling 'holy' bread and ale. At Croscombe almost every section of the community seems to have been involved and in a way which suggests that subtle social pressure was as effective as ecclesiastical sanction.

The social pressure came through the sort of gentle rivalry still apparent among stall-holders at a modern church fête. The rival groups in Croscombe were those representing the working population of the parish, the hogglers or farm labourers, the weavers and the tuckers or fullers. Added to those were the maidens, the young men (sometimes called 'yonglens') and the wives. Each group was given a 'stock' at the beginning of the year, a small sum in part spent on lights burning in some part of the church with which the group was particularly associated. Like the biblical servants given talents, each group was expected to return at the next annual accounting with an increase.

At the audit for the year 1474-5 the tuckers and the weavers, each given a stock of 12d, produced an extra 11d, the hogglers produced 10d to add to their original 2s, the young men brought an additional 2s 2d. In the next year the weavers produced 10d, the hogglers 1s 10d, the tuckers 1s 10d, the young men 3s 9d but the maidens, perhaps in only their first attempt, just 9d. The weavers fell by the wayside after a few years, several times recording 'nowghte', but the other groups continued well into the 1530s, in 1531–2 raising between them 25s 9d, most of which was achieved by the maidens.

There were other, more public ways of raising money in Croscombe in the 1470s, such as regular Easter and Michaelmas processions and the rather more secular Robin Hood or King's Revel. And, of course, there were other sources of income such as bequests and gifts. In 1478–9, for instance, the wardens received 4s in house rent, a bequest of 12d, gifts of 6s 8d and two silver rings, and some cloth for the high altar. There were also regular offerings at funerals (dead money) kept in a special box, and an even larger sum for more general offerings called the 'croke', presumably by its name an iron or earthenware vessel which was apparently taken on some sort of procession during which the wardens provided cheese.

Croscombe: *former church house*

The Croscombe accounts have far more detail about income than about expenditure. In 1478–9 there is reference to 'a bill of divers costs' for the large sum of £9 13s 4d, but there is no way of knowing for certain what building work was carried out. In 1480–1 the wardens paid nearly £11 to a carpenter and to several masons to build the church house, which still stands on the north side of the church. In January 1513 it was recorded that they had spent £27 11s 8d, described as 'the cost of the George', presumably not just the image of St George made by an Exeter freemason John Carter but also the chapel on the north side of the chancel, now used as a vestry, in which the statue was to be placed. Once established, the statue itself became the focus of a cult for which money was raised by organising processions, brewing a special ale, and handing round a collecting box.

The outer doorway of the south porch shows that the fabric of the present building dates at least from the late thirteenth century and the style of the nave arcades from the fourteenth century. Some years before the accounts begin there had evidently been a major rebuilding which involved the clerestory and a new nave roof. Two bosses in the waggon roof bear the six roses which were the arms of the Palton family, lords of the manor from the early fourteenth century until the death of Sir William Palton in 1450. Sir William, as befitted the lord of the manor, was buried in the chancel, but five years later his widow was licensed by the bishop to remove his body to the new chapel at the east end of the

Croscombe: *pulpit* Croscombe: *treasury*

south aisle, which had been built with money he had left.

The churchwardens' accounts of 1510 refer to a vestry, probably part of the new two-storeyed addition at the south-west angle of the church, providing a secure place for the church's valuables. Another addition to the fabric, but not mentioned in the accounts presumably because the wardens did not pay for it, was the battlemented parapet of the chancel which bears over the east gable the name of John Coumb, rector from 1473/4 to 1490.

Wills of two parishioners tell a little more: that by 1496 the church had a staff of 'several' parish chaplains, and that by 1507 one of the aisles was known as the Holy Trinity aisle and that in it stood a figure of St James the Apostle. In 1512 a third parishioner, John Inge or Yng, left a pipe of woad to be sold for the benefit of the fabric.

One other source reveals an addition not mentioned in the accounts. Richard Maudelyn or Mawdley, a Croscombe clothier, promised Robert Carver the sum of £10 if he would make a rood loft within two years. Robert failed although he had accepted £2 as an earnest. At some time in the 1490s Richard petitioned the king's chancellor for satisfaction. A rood loft was certainly constructed, for in the north wall is the stone staircase which led to it.

During the sixteenth century the manor of Croscombe passed to the Fortescue family of Filleigh in Devon. The manor house just north of the church, already partly divided by the Paltons, was let. In Queen Mary's reign the rector was forced to leave the parish and at least sixteen people were buried without proper rites for lack of a replacement. At the same time someone took over the church house. These and other examples of neglect were followed by some signs of recovery.

The great, two-tiered screen has been variously described as a 'proud, exotic structure', 'gloriously tall ... a fine big achievement'. With its pendants, obelisks and strapwork it is not what Richard Maudelyn had in mind in the late fifteenth century. He would have preferred a representation of Christ on the Cross to the Arms of James I, but his was not then a State Church. This screen, bearing the arms of the Fortescues, is more a statement of family loyalty to the Anglican Church than a contribution to liturgical proprieties. Yet the tall pulpit with its fantastical sounding board bearing the date 1616 and the arms of the newly-consecrated Bishop Lake, is a statement that here the Word was to be preached with power.

In the summer of 1936 the slender spire of Croscombe church was struck by lightning. The whole structure had to be taken down and rebuilt and the tower and belfry repaired. The task was enormous, but just as the people of the parish had contributed so magnificently towards the tower and spire as well as towards the rest of the building in the centuries before the Reformation, so now they responded and the tower and spire stand safe.

Churchwardens Accounts (S.R.S. iv), 1–48; P.R.O. C1/215/20 (rood loft contract); *Register of Thomas Bekynton* (S.R.S. xlix), 249–50.

Built for the Liturgy
TAUNTON, *St Mary Magdalene*

Material prosperity, especially noticeable in the cloth-making towns of the diocese at the end of the Middle Ages, and developments in popular attitudes to worship brought about changes in church buildings and furniture in the years immediately before the Reformation. Those developments had to do both with making space and filling it, creating room for liturgical movement in the form of processions and plays and dividing the eastern end of nave and aisles with parclose screens to form separate chapels, bringing worshippers closer to the celebrating priest than had been possible when Mass was sung at the distant high altar.

Chancel, nave, aisles and tower at St Mary's all appear at first sight to be part of a concerted plan of the later Middle Ages, but the arcade separating the two north aisles belongs to the thirteenth century, suggesting either a church which, unusually for the date, was already double-aisled; or, more likely, that the present inner north aisle was the earlier nave. A workman who fell from a beam in the church in 1240 may well have been employed on its alteration.

The impressive tower, a faithful copy (by Sir Giles Gilbert Scott and Benjamin Ferrey, 1858–62) of the original, is not preparation enough for the great space within, although worshippers would normally have come in through the great south porch into one of the two outer aisles, in fact into a square space divided by four arcades.

Until 1308 the church was dependent on Taunton's Augustinian priory, but in that year its vicar assumed responsibility for a number of churches near the town and the building itself became a focus of Taunton civic pride. The wills of leading townsfolk survive from the fifteenth century and tell the fascinating story of changes in the building and its use, most paid for by the dyers, fullers, clothiers and merchants whose cloth was making the town so prosperous.

By the 1480s parishioners had formed two brotherhoods, each with its own chapel and funds: one was dedicated to the Holy Cross, whose altar stood probably in front of the screen beneath the Rood which dominated the whole church. The other, with its chapel perhaps on the other side of the chancel entrance, was the Holy Sepulchre brotherhood. Further north or south at the end of each aisle, were altars dedicated to St Nicholas, St Katherine, the Holy Trinity and the Name of Jesus; and beyond the screen the chapels of Our Lady and of St Andrew. All those altars were generously endowed by Taunton's business community, sometimes with cash, sometimes with their own products – lengths of cloth, pipes of woad, wine, iron and items of clothing.

Taunton: *St Mary's church tower*

Taunton: *St Mary's church south porch, 1508*

Some 'new work' was evidently going on in 1498 which cannot now be identified, but subsequent bequests were for a processional way and a new aisle. John Tose by a will dated 1501 left the large sum of 40 marks (£26 13s 4d), together with a further 20 marks (£13 6s 8d) left by his father, towards the building of an 'ambulatory' or procession way before the Holy Sepulchre altar. No other surviving wills mention this particular work, but in 1508 John Togwell left a pipe of wine or 40s 'to the building of the new work in the south part of the church', almost certainly the present outer south aisle. The great south porch was built at the same time for the date 1508 appears on the right side of the entrance. Alison Togwell, John's widow, left money to the new work and also willed that a chapel of St George be 'built in the best manner' where the saint's statue already stood.

Meanwhile, between 1488 and 1505 other legacies were being received for the tower and its progress can be charted: in 1502 Richard Best gave cash for pinnacles; Agnes Burton in 1503 provided glass for a 'gable window'; in 1514 William Nethway paid for the tracery of two more tower windows.

Three other wills tell more of the story of parish life. John Nethway's executors in 1503 gave cash for a wooden cross with a stone base to be erected in the churchyard beside the procession way there. In the same year Agnes Burton left to the 'Sepulchre service' a red damask mantle and another lined with silk 'to th'entent of Mary Magdaleyn Play'; to be used, in other words, for the Easter drama, a re-enactment of the discovery of the Resurrection made by the church's patron.

In 1537 Joan Tedbury left 40s to build a church house on condition that the work was actually started before the money was paid: a rather late date for such a project. Only a year later prayers for the dead were officially declared invalid and all money left to endow masses at most of the altars in the church was confiscated, the brotherhoods dissolved, the guild of Our Lady swept away. For a few years the church must have seemed rather bare without colourful vestments, lights, images, the 14 clergy and the action of the Mass. The High Cross was restored with the Mass after 1554 but from 1559 the church was a preaching house for a form of worship based on a formal liturgy and the exposition of the Word of God.

Taunton: *St Mary's church Magdalene Centre, 1993*

In the late seventeenth and the eighteenth centuries the parish had to compete with strong nonconformist elements in the town and despite the appointment of at least one eminent preacher the church rather lost the initiative. The building came to life again in two campaigns of restoration, in 1843–4 and 1868–72. Box pews and a great pulpit in the middle of the north arcade were removed, the chancel floor was raised to give prominence to choir stalls and altar, and over some sixty years architects and craftsmen tried to restore with images, stained glass, encaustic tiles and paint something of the medieval splendour of St Mary's. The twentieth century has added its own contribution including in 1985 a nave altar and in 1993 a suite of rooms designed by Michael Stancliffe. Thus today's church has again brought the altar back among the people and provided some of the practical facilities offered by the old church house.

Somerset Medieval Wills (S.R.S. xvi, xix, xxi); *The Life of Richard Kidder*, D.D. (S.R.S. xxxvii), 97; J. Cottle, *Some Account of the Church of St Mary Magdalene, Taunton*; W.H. Askwith, *The Church of St Mary Magdalene, Taunton.*

Generous Patrons
NORTH CURRY, *St Peter and St Paul*

~❦~

The royal manor of North Curry passed by charter of Richard I in 1189 to the dean and chapter of Wells, part of the endowment arranged for his rapidly rising cathedral by Bishop Reginald FitzJocelin. The connection with Wells is still maintained through the dean who is patron of the living.

Of the church standing in Bishop Reginald's time only the north doorway survives, with its characteristic zig-zag decoration, but the massive central tower, built about 1300, probably replaced an earlier one. Evidence for rebuilding then are the cusped Y-traceried windows of the tower's lower stage, the old roof-lines of the nave and south transept, a lancet in the tower stair turret, the plain, double-chamfered western arches of the transepts, and the rere-arches of the south transept windows. The chancel was presumably also rebuilt at the same time, for the east window is of five cusped and stepped lancets.

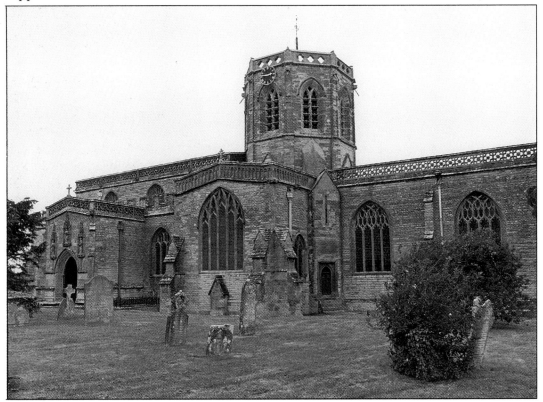

North Curry: *exterior*

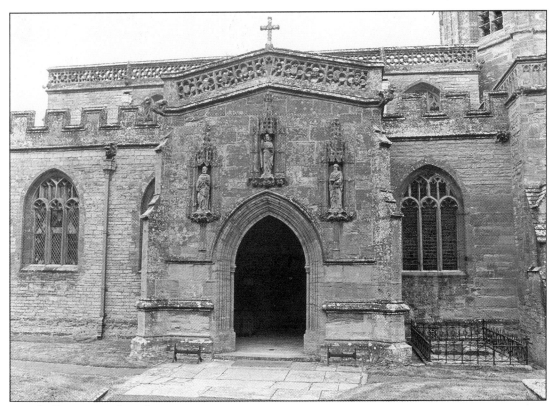

North Curry: *south porch*

Major work was done in the nave in the second quarter of the fourteenth century, for there are traces of two Decorated windows above the north arcade of the nave, witness to a clerestory. New aisles were built soon afterwards, and within a century the church had begun to acquire its Perpendicular character. It would be too much to hope that the three surviving churchwardens' accounts, for 1443–4, 1445–7 and 1460–1, would record major building work, but in each there are references to minor repairs and alterations: in 1443 William Helier of Taunton was paid for whitening and washing the building, using sand from Currymoorsford and lime bought at Bathpool. In 1445–7 masons repointed the walls, in the second account 2d was spent on an 'ostio called a wyndowe' inserted in the bell tower, and there were minor repairs to glass and to the north aisle roof. More money was spent on a new church stile and repairs to the churchyard wall using topping stone from Curry Mallet. In 1460–1 the largest outlay on building was for timber for the south aisle and some more wall topping, this time bought in Bridgwater and presumably brought up the Parrett.

There were, of course, other expenses: in one year two silver cruets and two silver candlesticks. Building works, repairs and the cost of vestments, bells and ornaments all had to be paid for from the wardens' own funds. Those came from gifts in cash and kind, 1s a year from the wardens of Stoke St Gregory for a nominal share of the upkeep of the churchyard, bells and tower, whatever could be saved by good housekeeping in the form

85

of sales of sand and lime left over from the whitewashing, loppings from the churchyard trees, even the old church stile. But most cash every year, as in other parishes, came from the profits made from the ale made for the patronal festival.

Most visitors to the church come from the market place through the churchyard and see at first a great Perpendicular church: octagonal tower, pierced and embattled parapets, clerestory, and magnificent three-, four- and five-light windows of golden Ham stone lighting nave, transept and chancel. The broad porch includes three fine, though empty, niches, and a fan vault.

It might seem all of a piece, the work of a single designer. That cannot be proved for no details are known of the latest changes to the nave and aisles; but the date and cost of the chancel, or rather the major costs of the chancel, are known exactly. Repairs were the responsibility not of the churchwardens but of the lords and patrons of North Curry, the dean and chapter of Wells. Ever since 1234 the chapter had taken most of the tithes paid in the parish and appointed a vicar on a relatively small income to serve the cure. Perhaps as a result of the large amounts spent by the parish the contrast between the two parts of the church became very noticeable. At a meeting in Wells in 1502 the chancel was actually described as 'totally ruined' so the chapter decided to appoint their treasurer, Master Thomas Harries, to organise its rebuilding; a room in Curry was set aside for him and hay was provided for his horses; and he had to pay the workmen, collecting the total cost, £52 13s 8d, from chapter income over the next four years.

It is not certain what work was entailed; certainly the great Ham stone windows and much more, but perhaps not a new roof, for repairs to the leadwork were recorded in 1504–5 and 1507, and the battlements were paid for separately by the chapter in 1504-5 and by Canon Peter Carsleigh of Wells in 1506.

Churchwardens Accounts (S.R.S. forthcoming); *Wells Cathedral Manuscripts,* i and ii; Wells Cathedral, Liber Ruber, f. 99.

The Squire and his Relations
STAWLEY, *St Michael*

~❧~

H enry Howe of Stawley was well known between Wellington and Tiverton, a sheep farmer or clothier, probably both, who supplied the raw materials or the finished cloth for which the district was famous in the early years of the sixteenth century. His parish church, rather nearer Wellington and just within the diocese of Bath and Wells, stands on a rounded grassy hill from which scattered farms can be seen in all directions, for it is a countryside of farmsteads and not villages.

When Henry Howe began to make his money his church comprised just a nave and chancel, the nave already ancient, for stones on the north side were laid in Norman herringbone fashion. The chancel was built in the thirteenth century, the south wall of the nave in the fourteenth. In that last rebuilding the craftsmen re-used the old door and its fine ironwork still remains. The nave roof was renewed in the fifteenth century, partly paid for by members of the Poulett family whose coat of arms, three swords in pile, are on the easternmost boss.

Pouletts were both lords of the manor and patrons, but they lived miles away in Hinton St George. A Poulett may have contributed to the cost of the tower, for the swords are to be seen there, too; but the main donor was Henry Howe. His name and that of his wife Agnes are carved in stone, partly in reverse, on a scroll above the west door: *Pray for the sowle of Henry Howe and Agnes his wyffe, anno domini MCCCCCXXIIJ.*

Stawley: *inscription over west door, 1523*　　**Stawley:** *interior*

Stawley: *exterior*

Five years later Henry Howe drew up his will. It was conventional enough, its main part leaving small sums to Wells cathedral, to the friars, to his godchildren, to his parish priest. The witnesses included the rector of his parish and two members of his own family; Agnes was to be his sole executrix. And he asked for burial within the tower he had built, a fitting place for a founder.

Some time later he wrote a codicil, giving specific directions for the commemoration of his death: 18d to be paid by his next heir each year to maintain a lamp on the north side of Stawley church – perhaps where he had owned a seat – and another light at Luxborough. In addition 18 churches between Tiverton and Hillfarrance, north as far as Chipstable, south to Sampford Peverell, should each receive 6s 8d or 3s 4d to remember him. Henry Howe was dead by February 1529.

The light in Stawley has long since gone out but Howe's memorial is that sturdy tower and the request for prayer which few will now be able to interpret. The question of lights came up at Stawley a few years later, just before the Reformation changes caused the poor parishioners such confusion. In 1547 the parson seems to have been something of a miser. He was supposed to find two tapers on the high altar in the church but he did not permit them to be lighted, and 'when they are lyghted by the clarke the person blowyth them owte agayne'.

Henry Howe would hardly recognise the interior of the church he so adorned, but it is a striking rarity, furnished in the taste of the eighteenth and nineteenth centuries and preserved by a man for whom the modern world of his day had few charms. For thirty-seven years until his death in 1879 John Hayne stood under that elegant canopy and preached as he was in duty bound. From 1845 he rode over each Sunday afternoon to Raddington to do duty there. And it is still remembered of him that on weekdays he rode to hounds dressed in his cassock and carrying an umbrella.

During those thirty-seven years no restorer was allowed near Stawley; the eighteenth-century communion rails, the early nineteenth-century pews, the table of command-ments, the creed and the Lord's Prayer were the latest additions permitted.

John Popham Hayne, one of his two equally eccentric sons, succeeded his father as rector of Stawley in 1879 and remained rector for fifty years. Haynes were patrons as well as rectors; as well known in the district as Henry Howe so many years before. Not exactly squires, but as influential in a country where men were squires who farmed wide acres and were generally looked up to. Stawley is still squire country and the visitor will see just inside the churchyard the grave of yet another, Squire Batten of Kittisford Farm, 1911–91; another in a long line dating back to Henry Howe and beyond.

Somerset Medieval Wills 1501–30 (S.R.S. xix), 270.

Pressures of Change
WELLS, *St Cuthbert*

~⇜✦⇝~

S t Cuthbert, the great apostle of the North, was King Alfred's favourite saint and the dedication of Wells's first parish church gives a clue to its origin. Its fine tower, elegant above the Victorian terrace, is often the visitor's first experience of Wells and many have mistaken it for the cathedral. As the parish church of medieval Somerset's largest town, St Cuthbert's is evidence of the means and the devotion of its parishioners. From its origin it was well endowed, so well that a share of its income was appropriated, to use the technical term, to the general funds of the cathedral.

From 1136 Bishop Robert's new cathedral chapter was to be endowed with, among other property, some land which Bishop Godfrey had given to St Cuthbert's at its dedication. In 1240 Bishop Jocelin allowed the cathedral an even larger share, giving the whole endowment of the living to the canons, but requiring them in return to appoint a 'competent' vicar to serve the cure for them. Competent implied an adequate stipend as well as ability, but part of the deal by the mid fourteenth century included an annual payment by the vicar of £13 6s 8d to the canons. In return the canons made themselves responsible for the fabric of the chancel, and in the years 1342–4 gave over £40 for its rebuilding.

Part of the shaft of a twelfth-century pillar piscina now in the Lady Chapel is a visible reminder in the present church of the dedication of the earlier one by Bishop Godfrey (bishop 1122–35). The form of the columns in the nave – square with four groups of triple shafts – belong to the thirteenth century, the time of Bishop Jocelin and the work of men who also worked on the cathedral. They built a large church here with a central tower and transepts, but they did not build high enough for all tastes. Two centuries later, when Wells masons like their fellows elsewhere were sacrificing all to light, they removed the nave roof and its arcades, added 11 feet to the pillars and put the arcades back again. Above they built a clerestory and finally carpenters added a stunning roof. Aisles were similarly raised in proportion and windows totally replaced. And to the west was built a fine tower and a fine tower arch. Heraldry on the tower points to building beginning before 1411 and finishing about 1430. By that time the nave would have been completed.

That was not the end of the work, for in each transept are the remains of reredoses, that in the south made by John Stowell, a Wells freemason, in 1470. Both were rediscovered in 1848 during the course of restoration, very badly damaged by men who wanted to destroy such traces of the Old Religion during the course of the Reformation. The panelled ceiling in St Cuthbert's chapel was similarly hidden, though not destroyed, and

Wells: *St Cuthbert's church interior*

Wells: *St Cuthbert's church tower*   **Wells:** *Tree of Jesse*

was only found again in 1960. The whole church was, so to say, at the sharp end of the religious changes not because its people had extremes of view but simply because the parish was at the centre of diocesan government, the bishop or his officials rarely very far away. Parish reactions to the religious changes demanded by the bishop – and of him by the Crown – were crucial.

Perhaps the changes directed by Bishop Barlow under Edward VI had been popular – the end of the Mass and elaborate liturgies, the end of chantries and prayers for the dead, and with them the carved reredoses of yesteryear. But on the very day of Queen Mary's proclamation of the restoration of the Mass, the vicar had no hesitation. On that day 'Mass was solemnly sung in the parish church of St Cuthbert according to the old use.'

But at least one member of the congregation, Thomas Lygh, was unhappy. Just after the second lesson at Mattins, before the Prayer Book had been abandoned, he noticed two lighted candles and a painted crucifix on the high altar and shouted out to the priest: 'what the devill have we heere, are we going to set up idolytre agen ?' He soon found himself complained of directly to the Queen and the whole incident was duly recorded by the clerk of the city corporation.

Bishop Bourne, Queen Mary's nominee to the see of Bath and Wells, held his first visitation in St Cuthbert's on 3 July 1554, nearly a year after Lygh's outburst. Master James Bounde STP preached the sermon and among those cited to appear before the court were John Thorne, who had refused to acknowledge the Host at the elevation, and John Stone who did not believe in prayers for the dead. Stone changed his mind when summoned to the cathedral and had to recant publicly before the vicar of St Cuthbert's. Two glovers had not been attending church since Mass had been restored, two local innkeepers and a brewer seem to have offered meals and drinks during service time and did not much hold with fish on Fridays; and one woman would not go in procession and venerate the sacrament.

Three years later the bishop's officers returned to St Cuthbert's. In many more remote parishes wardens were accused of failing to build stone altars, or restore service books and tabernacles. At St Cuthbert's, as at many others, the Mary and John, the figures of the crucified Christ and his supporters, had not been restored. But here there was a good reason. The wardens reported faithfully that they had a crucifix but 'dare not set up the same for the fere of the styple which is in decay'. And they clearly knew best, for in 1561 the city corporation set up a fund 'for the newe makynge and settynge vppe the Churche whare the styple did stand'. The steeple had, in fact, come crashing down. The inhabitants of High Street, Chamberlain Street, Cuthbert Street and Southover together raised £55 5s 8d. as the first stage of their restoration campaign. Perhaps those daring alterations to the building a century or so before had caused a fundamental weakness. The restoration scars in the nave can still be seen in the pieces of flat wall east of the nave arcade and in front of the chancel arch, made bare where masons cut off the original decorations.

Structural damage could be put right, but the abrupt theological and liturgical changes called the Reformation clearly proved unsettling to many. Seventy years after the tower fell down there was more trouble. Ale was being sold in the church house but, more serious, some parishioners with a drum and other instruments had become rather over-enthusiastic about a maypole and put it up while the bell was ringing for Sunday morning prayers, and again before evening prayers. Maypoles were, of course, not approved of by the puritan element in the Church but the king was determined to defend them. The problem with the maypole at St Cuthbert's was that it was used during service time, and the king could hardly defend such a proceeding.

As was entirely proper, the ringers celebrated in the correct manner when Thomas Ken came to Wells as the new bishop in May 1685, but a month later joy had given way to pain. Payments by the wardens to the ringers tell the story:

> paid the ringers for ringing the thanksgiving day for the victory over the rebels
>   [erased]
> paid for the ringing in the duke of Somersett ...
> and for the overthrow of James Scott ...
> and at the taken of James Scott ...

paid the ringers for the Thanksgiven day ...

paid the ringers for ringin my Lord Cheif Justice and the rest of the Judges ...

But was this rejoicing ? The warden noted after the first three entries that the mayor had paid the ringers' charges, and it seems that the judges paid for their own welcome. The attitudes were political, not necessarily those of the parish and the parishioners. Surely some of them had sympathy for the captive rebels herded into the church after the battle of Sedgemoor and kept there until Jeffreys and his fellows had meted out such justice as they pleased. The bill for fumigating the building tells its own story.

T. Serel, *Historical Notes on the Church of St Cuthbert in Wells; A Wells Miscellany*, S.R.O. D/P/wells st.c 4/1/1.

A Trace of Intolerance
KINGSTON ST MARY, *St Mary*

~⚜~

A nother wonderful tower, Quantock red sandstone with golden Ham stone dressings, overlooking a village nestling among green hills. A tower topped with battlements of pierced quatrefoils and arcading, pinnacles above niches, pinnacles beside belfry lights, pinnacles on angle buttresses, pinnacles on angle shafts. One small detail in all this embellishment is a particular form of the diamond stop bar or sill beneath the windows. It is to be seen at nearby Bishops Lydeard and Staple Fitzpaine, a little further away at Westonzoyland and Middlezoy. On the strength of this feature, the style of the transomed tower windows and other details, Kingston's tower is thought to have been built before 1490.

The south porch matches the tower in its ornate decoration; its delicate niches, a four-centred arch and a fan vault suggest an addition of about 1520, part of a major renovation of the whole of the east end of the building which may have involved the removal of a central tower as well as the rebuilding of the chancel and the north and south chapels at the end of each aisle. There is, of course, no proof of a central tower, but the nave arcades with their heavy circular piers and double-chamfered arches belong to an aisled building of the thirteenth century in which a crossing tower seems entirely likely.

So, early in the sixteenth century money was being lavished on a new chancel and chapels. A new chancel is, on the face of it, unlikely when the cost should have fallen on Taunton priory, an institution known in the case of the rebuilding of Bishops Hull church for its attempt to spend as little money as possible. Perhaps the prosperous farmers and clothiers of Kingston, supported by the two gentry families who owned the two aisles, decided on some compromise with the priory. Most other parishes would have rebuilt their nave to match the tower.

But if the parish left the fabric of the nave untouched, they furnished it lavishly. The carved bench ends are among the glories of the church, incorporating in their leaf and tracery designs a rosary, a pair of oxen with their yokes, and a weaver's shuttle with the date 1522. In addition there was a screen across nave and aisles, only a recess on the north side surviving to show the entrance to the rood loft.

One other small piece of carving seems to have escaped notice, and yet it illustrates the course of the Reformation in Kingston after Henry VIII's break with Rome. Just beside the font, itself probably brought in when the great rebuilding was going on, is a damaged shield once bearing the symbols of the Passion, the Five Wounds of Christ. The damage was almost certainly deliberate, as traces of the Old Religion were swept away, though it

Kingston St Mary: *tower*

Kingston St Mary: *damaged carving by font*

is curious that the same symbols on the font are preserved. In the years of extreme Protestantism under Edward VI the Rood would have been taken down from the screen, the stone altar removed and replaced by a wooden table for the communion, superfluous vestments, outmoded service books and unnecessary plate sold or given away by government order.

In 1554, when Queen Mary came to the throne, the policy was reversed: queen and bishop between them ordered the restoration of the Mass. When enquiry was made at Kingston, essential books were missing, the altar was covered in wax, vestments had not been replaced, no one would pay for the bread and wine for the Mass, and none would undertake to be churchwarden. Three years later, books and a chalice were still lacking and the Rood had not been replaced. People blamed the new owners of the chancel, the dean and chapter of Bristol, a body only founded in 1542 with the new diocese and but poorly endowed.

The dean and chapter of Bristol are still patrons of Kingston, and the church includes examples of artistic work from most centuries since the sixteenth: a seventeenth-century chalice, a locally made pulpit (1742) and a fine brass chandelier made by Thomas Bayley of Bridgwater in 1773. The need for improved music brought a organ, and hence an organ chamber, in 1867. The latest addition (1995) is the glass in the south window of the sanctuary by Julie Hibbert. Its reference in broken patterns in each light to man's inhumanity to his fellow man seems gloriously overcome by the mantle of Mary protecting the poor and persecuted, the black and white clasping hands of racial concord and the healing hands for so long associated with Kingston parish.

H.F. Ellis, *The Parish Church of Kingston St Mary.*

A Family Mausoleum
RODNEY STOKE, *St Leonard*

~❧~

The Rodneys came to this village on the Mendip scarp when Sir Richard Rodney married Maud, the daughter and heiress of the last Osbert Giffard, in or before 1316. They were already a family of some substance and several of them had perished in the service of the Crown: one died on his way to plead King John's cause at Rome; one fell at the siege of Acre during the Third Crusade; two were killed fighting for Henry III against the Welsh. The largest family estate, at Backwell, had been acquired by an even more remote ancestor who had supported the cause of the Empress Matilda against Stephen.

For thirteen generations from Sir Richard, Rodneys served as their social status demanded – as sheriff, justice of the peace, M.P. They married into local families of their own class and were, given potential problems of succession, a fortunate family, building up and retaining land which included property at Backwell, Saltford, Twerton, Hallatrow, Dinder, Badgworth and elsewhere. Sir Walter Rodney (died 1467) seems to have lost some influence because of his Lancastrian sympathies (his wife was a Hungerford) but the only obvious sign was not loss of land but removal from the roll of justices. As landowners the Rodneys were patrons of two livings, Backwell and Saltford, though the men they presented to the bishop for institution are not known to have been particularly distinguished representatives of their calling. In other words, so far as is known the Rodneys do not seem to have been more than conventionally religious, although in 1395 Sir John Rodney went into partnership with a Dorset landowner, buying a new ship based at Lyme whose purpose was to take pilgrims to the famous shrine of Compostella in northern Spain.

A few surviving family wills bring the Rodneys a little closer. John Rodney, son of the pilgrim tour operator, seems to have preferred Backwell to Stoke and left £6 13s 4d to the church fabric fund. When he made his will his wife was expecting a child and his heir Walter was still very young. Thus he left John Walsh, rector of Saltford, and another man as trustees and they were instructed in the event of the deaths of both his children to spend most of his ready cash for the good of his soul. John may well have been buried at Backwell; his son Walter certainly was when he died in 1467 and there is his effigy, in the north chapel, a knight in armour. No will of Sir Walter survives but his wife was left by her father a silver gilt figure of the Virgin with the Hungerford arms under her feet.

After Sir Walter's time the family seem to have preferred Rodney Stoke and the tombs of Sir Thomas (died c. 1471), his son Sir John (died 1526), Sir Edward (died 1657) and his wife and Sir Edward's son George and his wife are all there. Sir Thomas, like his father ,

Rodney Stoke: *family tombs*

lies in armour to signify social status. The figures on the sides of the tomb chest – Christ, the Virgin, St Anne and St Erasmus – may be conventional piety and may reflect either his own wishes or those of his family; it is impossible to be sure. Sir John probably rebuilt the manor house at Stoke and the principal witness to his will was Richard Carter, the rector.

The will itself is remarkably terse: 40s to the church where he should be buried, 40d to the cathedral at Wells, two personal bequests and the rest to his widow. Sir John's grandson and successor, also John, preferred Backwell to Stoke and had interests through his wife in many other parts of the country. His will, dated 1548, shows him conventional enough: cash bequests for the rector of Stoke and the clergy of Backwell for tithes forgotten. In addition, however, he gave the rent of six cows which he had let to a farmer at Stoke for the benefit of the poor of that parish, Draycott and Priddy, and at the end of the lease the cows were to form the marriage portion of six village girls.

Maurice, his son, was still a youngster when John died but he survived to serve as sheriff in 1580 and died in 1588. His only surviving son, George, died childless and the family estates passed to a distant cousin, another Sir John, who was probably the first member of his family to have an Oxford education. Sir Edward Rodney, who succeeded his

Rodney Stoke: *chancel screen and loft*

father in 1612, was one of seventeen children and himself had five sons but he amazingly proved to be the last of his line. His career was entirely typical: M.P. several times, justice of the peace and deputy lieutenant probably until the Civil War. During the war he was for the king, as any Rodney would have been, for was he not cousin to the marquess of Hertford who was the royalist commander in the West, and had not his wife been a member of the household of the late queen, Anne of Denmark ? The loss of his heir George in 1651 was clearly a great sorrow, only to be borne by the production of an image of his eventual resurrection in his homespun tomb. Sir Edward survived until 1657 and he and his sorrowing wife have a monument accompanied by angels.

There is more than a hint in St Leonard's church that Sir Edward's politics went hand in hand with his religion. The building is late medieval, the tower probably dating from the early part of the fifteenth century, the pierced parapet of the nave and north chapel perhaps a century later. The screen, pulpit and font cover (1625) and the altar table (1634) were no doubt entirely approved by the Laudian Bishop Piers. The screen is perhaps the most remarkable piece, for above it is a loft, surely not a rood loft but almost certainly a pew for the squire, reached through the former rood loft access in the north chapel. The bishops of Bath and Wells had had the right to appoint the parsons at Rodney Stoke for centuries, but Rodneys would surely make certain that what those

Rodney Stoke: *modern bench end*

parsons said and did was to their liking. From this screen parson and congregation could be dominated.

There were, of course, other branches of the Rodneys, one producing the great admiral, George Rodney (died 1792), not the first of his family to go to sea for Sir Edward's brother Henry was drowned off the coast of Africa. A similar fate befell Reginald Hale, one of the carvers of the fine modern pew ends in the church, who went down in the Titanic. Evelyn Coleridge Smith, one of the then rector's daughters, organised the local craftsmen, worthy successors to the carvers of Sir Edward's time. Evelyn and her sister Dora served as nurses abroad during the First World War from which they and all seventeen men and two other women from the parish came home safely.

Somerset Medieval Wills, 1383–1500 (S.R.S. xvi), 83–4; *1501–30* (S.R.S. xix), 227.

Defying the Bishop
BECKINGTON, *St George*

᠕᠍᠊ᠬᡟᡥᠬ᠍᠊᠊

Beckington, now mercifully free from the heavy traffic which once threatened to strangle it, may now be enjoyed again in the calm it deserves. Approached from the north, down the old road from Bath, the village reveals in its stone-tiled gables and mellow limestone something of its ancient prosperity. It stood strategically between the wool-producing areas of Salisbury Plain and the Mendips, and its houses and some of the details in its church reflect the success of Beckington clothmen.

Prosperity came early if the massive Norman tower is any indication. At the bell stage the openings have fine, zigzag mouldings and pairs of blank arches which some have seen as distant precursors of the great towers of the late Middle Ages. Some herring-bone masonry in the south wall of the chancel is all, otherwise, that remains of the early building which probably owed much to the Erleigh family, lords of the manor. The three shells on the family arms are to be found on the north arcade in the north aisle and continue the story of the family in the fourteenth century, the time of the knight and his lady lying in the chancel. Perhaps the knight is Sir John de Erleigh whose capture at the battle of Najera in Spain in 1367 cost his family a fortune in ransom. At the very end of the century a humble weaver's wife gave birth to a son Thomas who, probably taught first by the rector and then sent to Winchester, became one of the leading diplomats of his day before being appointed bishop of Bath and Wells. His family had no name so the boy took the name of his parish, and when he came to be bishop he seems to have preferred to use a rebus or badge rather than the expected coat of arms – a beacon formed from a barrel (tun) on a pole.

Prosperity in the fifteenth century passed to the people, although the brass commemorating John Seymour (died 1485) and his wife shows that landowners still had clout. The symbols on the brasses of John Compton (died 1510) and Thomas Webb (died 1585) were those which they used on their bales of cloth, and the profits they and their fellows made before the Reformation were lavished on their church. The nave was probably rebuilt c. 1470, the chapel at the east end of the south aisle c. 1510. The tower arch, the fan vault and the great west window both under the tower were also part of the remodelling scheme. Like many another church of a prosperous business community at the end of the Middle Ages, this too was furnished with four altars and four endowed and lighted images. Carved stone panelling at the east end of the north aisle and the rood loft stair are all that can now be seen of this magnificence.

A century later Beckington was known for its puritanism, and the contrast could not have been greater. Indeed, the parish, or rather its rector and wardens, became

Beckington: *tower*

nationally famous. At first the wardens and rector were not agreed on the matter. From 1594 Parson Walkwood was reported for refusing to wear a surplice, for not using the sign of the cross at baptisms, for not going with the wardens and parishioners on perambulation day, and for excessive preaching – twice on Sundays. The parson, in his turn, complained that the wardens had not bought the large copy of the Bible as required, and had not been very assiduous in compelling attendance at church.

Within the next twenty years or so the parish had gone far along the road of puritanism. Their communion table had been moved from its traditional position along the east wall and had been placed lengthways in the centre of the chancel, surrounded by a wainscot and kneeling bench. The change represented the difference between a ceremonial table whose position was close to that occupied by the pre-Reformation table of sacrifice of the Mass; and something much nearer a domestic table around which those sharing the meal could properly gather.

In 1635 James Wheeler and John Frye, the two churchwardens, were summoned to Wells by Bishop Piers, that ardent supporter of Archbishop Laud and the High Church revival. They had refused the bishop's order to move the table back to its original position. Having faced the bishop's wrath they still refused, were excommunicated and were finally sent to prison. The whole parish was behind them and in 1637 there was a riot in the churchyard, a 'fowle and insolent ryott ... to the great dishonour of church, government ... and to the evill example of others'. The rioters were fined, with the alternative of a humble and very public apology to the bishop. One man held out for nearly three years.

The rector himself was probably in general on the side of his parishioners. His name was Alexander Huish and he was a scholar of national stature. He upset some of his parishioners by altering the services and in 1640 he was arrested but bailed. He was described

as one of the 'vitious' clergy supported by Bishop Piers who was removed from his parish, imprisoned first in Wiltshire and later in London and still later fined. Perhaps during this time of exile he put the finishing touches to his part in the production of the Polyglot Bible, so called because the text is in nine languages and which appeared between 1654 and 1657. He was restored to Beckington in 1660.

R.W. Dunning, *The Church of St George, Beckington.*

Beckington: *merchant's mark*

Triumph out of Disaster
KEYNSHAM, *St John the Baptist*

O n 7 April 1403 John Jenys was instituted as perpetual vicar of Keynsham. His title meant not that he was there for ever, but that his income was a permanent endowment. He was evidently not content and soon raised the question of tithes with the patrons of the living, the abbot and convent of Keynsham, whose great monastic buildings stood east of his church. It is not known when the 'discords' between them began, but soon after the middle of November 1404 an agreement was reached and its terms were formally drawn up 'in a certain high chamber within the wall of the said monastery'.

The agreement defined the vicar's income for the future and incidentally it reveals a great deal about the size and character of the original parish of Keynsham. Tithes were payable from Keynsham itself and from the hamlets of Chewton Keynsham and Stockwood mostly in the form of agricultural produce but also in unspecified merchandise and handicrafts, showing that already there were traces of a market and also the beginnings of the town's long industrial tradition.

The vicar was also entitled thereafter to a house and some pieces of land near the abbey barn, to offerings in the parish church and in Chewton Keynsham chapel, and to two waggon-loads of hay and two of fuel. In return, with the help of a chaplain, he was to minister to the inhabitants of Keynsham itself and to those in the hamlets of Chewton Keynsham and Stockwood. The abbot and convent for their part agreed to pay chaplains in the rest of the parish at Queen Charlton, Publow, Filton (Whitchurch) and Brislington as well as at the oratory or small chapel at Newyke called St Anne in the woods. The whole vast area was several miles across in every direction and has the characteristics of a Saxon minster parish and before that of a Roman estate perhaps centred on the large villa found not far from the parish church.

The dissolution and destruction of Keynsham abbey in 1539 signalled the disappearance of the pastoral arrangement achieved with such care little more than a century before, and it gave an opportunity for Publow to become independent although Whitchurch and Brislington still continued in their dependent status in the late sixteenth century. The vicar of Keynsham concentrated as before on Keynsham itself and Chewton.

In 1626 the leading members of the parish were the three churchwardens, Robert Cox, Gregory Llewellen and Thomas Leman, and four questmen, Richard Holben, William Gregorye, John Walsh and Robert Ford. Those seven men or their successors and the new vicar, Thomas Tillie, were faced a few years later by a great disaster. In the late

Keynsham: *tower*

> tempestuous weather ... intermixed with hideous clapps
> of thunder and flashes of lightning ... by reason of
> the force thereof, in a moment threw down the steeple
> or spire of the Tower, which, with the fall thereof,
> crushed down likewise the greatest and principallest
> parte of the body of the said church, chancel, vestry,
> pulpit, and seates, and defaced the pavement also; and
> the tower being raised from the top to the foundation.

The 'very faire, large and substantiall Church and a great ornament to the sayd Towne' was thus 'most lamentably ruinated', and it was clearly far beyond the means of the inhabitants, 'men of small ability ... for the most part ... poore handicrafts men' to raise the £690 or £700 which repairs were thought to cost. Thus the lord lieutenant of the county, Lord Poulett, and the justices of the peace, sponsored a Brief – an official means of collecting cash after disasters in the name of the king – which was circulated in a wide area between Kent and Hereford, explaining the problem in the words quoted above. The Brief was issued on 16 January 1634, a year after the event and sufficient time to discover that the parish could not cope alone. Ever hopeful, the churchwardens had actually opened a special account on the day after the disaster.

That account was in the possession of the Revd H. T. Ellacombe in 1847, for he exhibited it to members of the Society of Antiquaries of London. It was described as 'very detailed' and showed sums collected and laid out between January 1634 and 1640. No trace of it has been found since, and its loss is much to be regretted. Was the work completed by 1640 (the new pulpit used to bear the inscription 'Blessed are they that have the word of Gode and kepe it 1634'), or are the dates 1654 on a bell and 1655 on the weathercock more significant ?

The spire which so damaged the church stood on a tower at the eastern end of the north aisle where the tower's lowest stage still stands. It was replaced by the present tower at the west end. Sir Stephen Glynne recognised it as 'in imitation of Perpendicular work' but considered there were 'strong indications of debased style', notably the belfry windows. In contrast he thought the panelling of the middle stage 'rather fine'. For Pevsner it is 'a remarkable achievement ... clearly meant to be a Somerset Gothic tower' in its use of set back buttresses, four-light west window, and Bristol-style parapet and pinnacles. The new west tower reflected the general Perpendicular character of the church, though it is clear that the chancel essentially dates from the thirteenth century and the south aisle has a ball-flower cornice beneath its parapet, indicating work of the later part of the same century and thus a large church at the time.

Edmund Buckle, the diocesan architect, was particularly struck by the proportions of the long, low nave, which he likened to a Roman basilica. He also drew attention to the fact

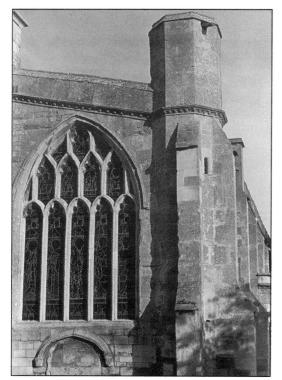

Keynsham: *part of west front*   **Keynsham:** *Bridges monument*

that the west end of the church still bore traces of a 'very beautiful' Perpendicular screen whose turrets still survive.

Part of the abbey estate, including ownership of the chancel and patronage, was acquired some years after the Dissolution by Thomas Bridges, and many of his successors were buried in that same chancel. The monuments to Sir Henry (died 1587) and Sir Thomas (died 1661) give some idea of the importance the family attached to themselves. The informative benefaction boards tell of the generosity of other members of the family, notably another Sir Thomas who died in 1706 at the age of ninety having founded a school, an almshouse and an annual sermon. His gift of a covered chalice and two flagons made by Philip Rolles in 1701 was as flamboyant as that of his wife, who gave a crimson velvet altar cloth and cushion and a crimson velvet pulpit cloth, all fringed in gold. Harry Bridges in 1725 gave the small font. The last member of the family to be buried in the vault died in the 1740s, for the property passed to the senior line, the dukes of Chandos, who lie in their church of Whitchurch or Little Stanmore. The last family link with Keynsham was Richard Plantaganet Campbell Temple-Nugent-Brydges-Chandos-Grenville, 3rd duke of Buckingham and Chandos, marquess of Buckingham, marquess of Chandos, earl Temple of Stowe, earl Nugent, viscount and baron Cobham. He was the last of the family to act as patron when he presented a vicar in 1854 and he and his family paid for the restoration of and reroofed the chancel in 1862.

A few years before that, in 1847, 'Churchgoer' visited the church and remarked on the 'ruinous' neglect of the building and noted in particular the north aisle, the home of the parish fire engine and of a stove whose chimney was fixed across two or three windows. Lady Bridges's pulpit cloth was 'frayed and faded', the Bible on the reading desk 'could not be said to have two whole covers' and the Book of Common Prayer, also give by Lady Bridges, 'seemed devotedly determined to share its fate'. The service was 'feebly and coldly performed' and 'melancholy and dispiriting in the extreme' although the sermon was 'very fair and sound'.

Restorations in 1861–3 by Benjamin Ferrey and in the late 1960s ensured that there were no further structural failures, but the rapid growth of Keynsham's population demanded structural changes of a different kind. The creation of the Keynsham Team Ministry in 1975 was, in a sense, a partial recreation of the ancient minster parish, for it combines Queen Charlton and Chewton Keynsham with the parish church, the church of St Francis (1957) and the formerly independent parish of Burnett.

Registers of Walter Giffard and Henry Bowett (S.R.S. xiii), 46–8; *S.D.N.Q.* viii. 267; *Archaeologia* xxxii. 445; *Proc. Som. Arch. Soc.* xlvii. 61–2; ibid. xlix. 144–5; J. Collinson, *History of Somerset*, ii. 403–11; *Churchgoer's Rural Rides.*

Publishers of Truth
LONG SUTTON,
Friends' Meeting House

*After a long night of apostacy ... the Lord
remembred his Covenant ... and in the yeere
one Thousand six hundred Fifty five sent
severall of his faythfull servants ... from
the Countyes of Westmorland and Lancaster ...
into the County of Somersett ... And in the
Yeare one Thousand six hundred Fifty and six
many people ... began to wayte on the Lord ...*

Thus was the story of the arrival of Quakerism at Street and 'severall other places'
written in the year 1659. The preaching of the 'faythfull servants' proved particularly effective in an area which had seen a resurgence of High Anglicanism in the years
before the Civil War, but which now found the Presbyterian and Baptist ministers
preaching in the steeple-houses no more acceptable. The new ministers still demanded
the ancient tithes and fees, the old respect for the parson and a liturgy of words. The new
preachers advocated silence and an end to social airs and graces.

There was a certain immodesty in their behaviour: two 'bore witness' in Cameley
steeple-house against a doctrine and a form of worship of which they did not approve.
Two more accosted the priest in the churchyard of St John's, Glastonbury and presented
him with a manifesto. Such attacks brought their own, often brutal, reward. Refusal of
the new Quakers to pay tithes or fees for weddings and burials let in the full panoply of
the law which after the return of bishops and Anglican paraphernalia at the Restoration
made them subject to excommunication in the ecclesiastical courts as well as heavy fines
in the civil courts. The search for and break-up of meetings for worship was the
inevitable response from the Anglican civil power.

By 1659 Quakers in the county had organised themselves: 45 men at a General Meeting
at Glastonbury decided that attacks (known as Sufferings) should be meticulously
recorded, that births, marriages and burials should be registered, that procedures should
be settled for matters of discipline and dispute, that education should be a priority and
that there should be financial support for poor members. Nine years later George Fox
met Friends at Ilchester and there settled the general pattern of government for Quakers
in the county based on three areas (Monthly Meeting) and a General (Quarterly)
Meeting. Keynsham was to be the first place at which members from 16 groups

(Meetings) in the north-east of the county should gather, Bridgwater for six groups in the centre and west, and Ilchester for 11 groups in the south. Among the southern group were Roger Slocombe, Thomas Gaylard, Robert Banton, Richard Nowell, Robert Ford, Edward Perris, Jacob Turner and William Thresher, members of a Meeting which gathered in homes in Long Sutton and Knole.

Those early Friends faced almost thirty years of persecution. In 1661 there were 209 in the county gaol at Ilchester after a particularly vicious outbreak of intolerance. Most were soon released, but there were still more than two dozen there in 1662. The Conventicle Act of 1670 brought raids on Meetings and further arrests, but 39 still at Ilchester in 1672 were released under the Declaration of Indulgence. There were 33 there in 1679, more were rounded up in 1682–3 and early in 1684, 83 were released. Some individuals, many of them the leaders of the movement, spent up to twenty years in Ilchester, but their incarceration was often little more than house arrest and much Quaker business was done at the overflow gaol called the Friary.

The strength of the Long Sutton Meeting can be gauged quite accurately. The group had been formed by 1662 and a year later the churchwardens reported that there were twenty 'sectaries' in the parish, most if not all Quakers, who refused to attend church,

Long Sutton: *Friends' meeting house exterior*

Long Sutton: *Friends' meeting house interior*

married each other without banns and buried their dead without licence. In 1669 a house at Knole was licensed for worship and 100 Quakers attended. In 1685, 42 people were reported for not attending church and probably as many as 37 of them were Quakers. For more than half a century these folk had no settled place of meeting: Robert Ford's house in Knole was in use by 1669 when the 'teachers' were those Quaker heavyweights John Anderdon, Christopher Bacon and Jasper Batt. In 1670 and again in 1689 Richard Nowell was the occupier of the building they used, and in 1699 Samuel Langfield. The meeting house still in use was built in 1717.

Some of those eight members of Long Sutton Meeting in 1668, men who were 'Friends of Truth ... meete to keep the mens Meetings' illustrate both the sufferings and the distinctive lifestyle of early Quakers. Roger Slocombe was a blacksmith by trade and married Jacob Thomas's daughter. In July 1685 he and his brother, who was not a Quaker, were arrested by the king's army a day or two before the battle of Sedgemoor and were accused of making scythes for the rebels. Roger denied the charge and his brother declared that the weapons he made were for the reasonable defence of his parish. Both were allowed home but Roger still had to convince imprisoned Friends in Ilchester since several others had compromised themselves in their sympathy for the rebel cause.

Richard Nowell lived in the house raided in 1670 when it was used for meetings and he lost all possessions the authorities could lay their hands on. Friends reasonably enough described him at the time as a poor man. Later on he was known as a husbandman. His wife died in 1681 and Elizabeth Pollett later went to stay with him until Friends persuaded her to leave. In 1690 Richard proposed marriage in strict Quaker form with Edith Samways, but Elizabeth objected and Friends supported her. Richard ignored their views and went to another Meeting where he and Edith 'pretended to take each other as husband and wife' and then returned to live in the meeting house at Long Sutton. Friends evicted them but they seem to have been forgiven and returned four years later. Elizabeth, 'her minde being thus drawn forth after a husband', married another man who was not a Quaker although 'shee knew that shee was in the way of destruction.'

Perhaps the most remarkable Quaker to be associated with Long Sutton was John Whiting (1656–1722), whose book *Persecution Exposed* tells much about Friends' experiences. The son of John and Mary Whiting of Nailsea, converts to the Truth in 1654, he was imprisoned for not paying tithes at the age of 23 and remained a prisoner until 1686. Several times he left Ilchester, once on a dangerous mission to Taunton when Monmouth was there, to persuade his future brother-in-law to leave. Prison was, in fact, the safest place for him, safer than the time he sat in a garden in Long Sutton on the day

Long Sutton: *Friends' meeting house, Court House*

after Sedgemoor while a justice of the peace sat in the house asleep. In 1686 he married Sarah Hurd of Long Sutton and took over her business as a linen draper before moving to Wrington and eventually to London.

The simple but elegant meeting house built in 1717 stands in a small burial ground and via a green walk through a garden leads to the medieval Court House, which also belongs to Friends. Its hipped roof, sash windows and plain wooden shutters are the antithesis of every Anglican steeple-house. Inside, one end of the building is occupied by a passage with a gallery above, both divided from the main meeting room by movable shutters. Original plain wooden benches are the only furniture; what more does the Truth need?

The Somersetshire Quarterly Meeting of the Society of Friends, 1668-99 (S.R.S. lxxv); G.L. Turner (ed.), *Records of Early Nonconformity*; *V.C.H. Somerset*, iii. 165.

Rational Belief

Taunton, Mary Street,
Unitarian and Free Christian

~⚜~

There is a old tradition, which can no longer be proved, that a group of Baptists was worshipping in woods near Hatch Beauchamp about 1630. Four years earlier there had been only five groups of Baptists in the whole country. Baptists from Hatch, Stoke St Gregory and Taunton were among those who formed an association at Wells in 1653, and while puritans were in the political ascendant, such folk, however strict their opinions, were on the whole free to worship in their own way.

The Restoration brought an inevitable Anglican backlash but the legal pains and penalties imposed on those who would not conform to the worship and doctrine of the Church as by law established both failed to destroy Baptists, Presbyterians, Quakers and Independents and provided in the form of court proceedings, surveys and licences much useful information for historians.

Thus, in 1669 a survey commissioned by Archbishop Sheldon of Canterbury revealed that in Taunton and its surrounding villages former Anglican clergy ejected from their livings in 1662 were both very active and prosperous. In Taunton itself six former Anglican clergy including George Newton and John Glanvill, former vicars of the two town churches, were preaching regularly in private houses to some 350 people, and other groups were active in Bridgwater and Oake. Some of these preachers had moved on by 1672 when some sort of temporary toleration was offered, but many more village groups had emerged and the houses of Edward Rossiter, William Gill and Thomas Stone in Taunton were duly licensed for worship.

It is impossible to say which of those groups was Baptist by persuasion, nor yet to discover how strong they were, both numerically and economically. A Baptist meeting suffered from the prevailing mood of intolerance in 1683 when it was sacked by the mayor, but following the Toleration Act of 1689 the 'Baptist New Meeting' was registered for worship in 1691 and was evidently rebuilt in a fashionable style reflecting the prosperity of its members in 1721. The imposing central pulpit and the large gallery provided the minister with a preaching theatre suitable for the times.

The earliest surviving trust deed of the chapel dated 1730 names four typical men of one of the West Country's largest manufacturing towns: Joseph Jefferies of Bishops Hull, clothier, Thomas Chester of Taunton, fuller, Thomas Jefferies of Taunton, sergemaker, and George Stone of Taunton, soap boiler. Four years later a new and larger trust was

Taunton, Mary Street: *interior*

formed: different men but of the same kind
– John Noble, a merchant from Bristol,
Ebenezer Jefferies, a sergemaker from
Bishops Hull, John Billett, a tobacconist
from Pitminster and from Taunton three
fullers, two sergemakers, a woolcomber, a
chapman, and a broker.

The new trust formed so soon after the first
may mark a significant change. The congregation, under the leadership of a forceful
minister and also perhaps inspired by the
secession of some disgruntled members of
the Independent Paul's Meeting, accepted
unorthodox views on the Trinity known as
Socianism or Arianism which emerged
from the prevailing interest in politics and
philosophy of the Age of Enlightenment.
The forceful minister was Joshua Toulmin,
who came in 1765 from a Presbyterian

Dr Joshua Toulmin

church at Colyton to lead what was then a small and declining congregation still holding Baptist opinions which he had recently adopted. He opened a school and his wife a bookshop in order to make a living. In 1769 Toulmin became an MA of the Baptist Brown University, Rhode Island, USA.

Perhaps a year later he adopted Socinianism and took his people with him. His liberal views were of little local interest until the disturbing events of the French Revolution and in 1791 he suffered much public odium but refused to leave and was one of the founders of the Western Unitarian Society in 1792. His many theological publications earned him the degree of DD from Harvard University, though he is perhaps best remembered in Somerset as author of the first history of Taunton. He left the town for Birmingham in 1803. (His son Harry, incidentally, served as a minister in Lancashire before emigrating to America in 1793 where he was successively president of the Transylvania college, Lexington, Kentucky, secretary for the state of Kentucky, judge in the Mississippi Territory and a member of the state assembly of Alabama).

In 1816 a new group of trustees included John Jefferies of London, continuing his family's interest in the cause, and Malachi Blake, a Taunton doctor. Such was the strength of local tradition that the church was still known locally as 'the Baptist Meeting-house' but 'now and for some years past' called Mary Street Chapel.

For a century thereafter many of Taunton's leading businessmen were members of the church and the trust of 1954 included two members of the Blake family. The impressive Sunday school building added beside the chapel, together with a new frontage for the chapel itself are evidence of the continuing prosperity of the cause into the early twentieth century. Today the tiny congregation, emphasising rather its Free Christian sympathies, welcomes preachers from many denominations to its monthly services and struggles to preserve its exquisite gem of nonconformity.

G.L. Turner (ed.), *Records of Early Nonconformity*; S.R.O. D/N/mst 2/1/1–8; *Dictionary of National Biography*.

TRUDOXHILL, *Congregational Chapel*

~*⚶*~

The notion of a permanent church building for a congregation which in 1669 worshipped under the leadership of John Ford and Robert Cox in Witham Friary would have been both illegal and impractical. They met instead in the houses of Joan Richards, Richard Yewins and William Clarke and they met illegally, defying the law which required their attendance at their parish church. Witham was a sensible place for such gatherings, for should a Somerset justice of the peace begin to take interest in them, they could without much difficulty cross over into Wiltshire for a while. Meetings in the woods of Maiden Bradley were still remembered two centuries later.

Ford and Cox were among many church leaders not willing to conform to the full doctrine of the Church of England, which had been returned to power after the Restoration. Some had been ejected from livings held during the Commonwealth, and among them was Henry Butler who in 1672, when for a time it was government policy to licence both preachers and meeting houses, cared for congregations at Maiden Bradley,

Trudoxhill: *Congregational chapel exterior*

Laverton, north of Frome, and at his former parish of Yeovil. Butler had an unusual career, having been educated at Harvard in New England, where his parents had emigrated from Kent in 1635, and who had come to be minister at Yeovil after a spell as schoolmaster at Dorchester, Massachusetts.

So the congregation formerly under Ford and Cox presumably went over to hear Butler at Maiden Bradley, and probably over the next fifteen years or so suffered the uncertainties if not the imprisonment which their minister experienced. During that time Butler seems to have moved to live at Witham and the congregation there made bold in 1688 to thank the king for his edict of toleration. That edict was turned into law by a more sympathetic parliament in 1689, and in that year Robert Smith's house at Witham was formally licensed as the meeting place of the Witham congregation. There for ten years Henry Butler ministered, until his death in 1696.

Perhaps because numbers grew, perhaps for other practical reasons, the congregation continued to move from time to time: to William Lush's house also in Witham, and to the houses of Thomas Sage and Thomas Yeoman in nearby Trudoxhill in 1698, possibly as alternatives. The house of Hugh Hooper at Witham was licensed in 1699, Nicholas Newport's in Trudoxhill in 1701, Robert Smith's in Nunney in 1702, William Smith's in Nunney in 1712.

And then in 1717 the little group under their minister Richard Jones of Nunney was evidently strong enough to settle down and build. Sixteen trustees, seven each from Witham and Nunney, one from Marston Bigot and one from Wanstrow acquired in the name of them all a cottage in Trudoxhill owned by Robert Newport on condition that within a year they would 'erect and convert the said cottage and premises into a hansom and convenient publick meeting house'.

Within that year they raised the sum of £149 19s 9d which paid for a conversion which externally kept the building's domestic face and even the datestone recording its original construction by Robert and Ann Newport in 1699. The inside was gutted to provide space for pews, pulpit and gallery. Twenty years on and a new group of trustees took

Trudoxhill: *Congregational chapel interior*

responsibility for a congregation drawn from many local villages including Upton Noble and Tytherington and from farmers and tradesmen including a woolcomber, a baker, a clothier and a maltster, typical both of the area and of the kind of social groups from which nonconformists came.

Some local opposition was induced by liquor at the Trudoxhill Revel but no theological disputes spoilt the apparently even tenor of this country congregation. David Hughes, minister for forty years, still lived at Nunney and ministered also to a church at Chapmanslade. David Watts, his successor, was ordained in the chapel in 1802 and less than a year later played host to the Wiltshire and East Somerset Congregational Association. He came to live in the village in 1812.

The nineteenth century probably saw the cause at its most successful and prosperous, with a Sunday school for 50 children, enough money raised to replace the box pews with new seats and a new pulpit, a stove to make the place more comfortable, and finally a new school room.

Such causes gradually lost their way when the State provided education; and the Church of England opened a mission church in the village in 1898. Less than a century later the church has become a private dwelling but the chapel is still a chapel, closed but at present preserved, a fitting memorial to the cause of Independency in this part of Somerset.

Calamy Revised, 93; G.L. Turner (ed.), *Records of Early Nonconformity*; M.McGarvie, 'Notes on Trudoxhill Chapel', *Frome Society Yearbook* 3. 54–62; R. Dunning (ed.), *Christianity in Somerset*, 63–5.

The Charity of Thomas Ken
GLASTONBURY, *St John the Baptist*

◈

The elegant late-medieval tower with its delicate pierced crown which stands proud above the town of Glastonbury and almost alone since the destruction of the abbey church, is yet another product of economic prosperity and flourishing religion in the years before the Reformation. Visitors to its light and elegant interior see a building of the late fifteenth century whose churchwardens have so fortunately preserved accounts of their building work, it must be said partly forced upon them by the removal of a great central tower after falling pinnacles warned of worse to come. The parallel with St Cuthbert's in Wells is thus remarkably close but rather better documented.

The nave arcades were totally rebuilt at Glastonbury, giving the impression of great space; and the large, five-light windows make the whole building lightsome, as Leland wrote. A fragment of a cusped window rere-arch of c. 1300 in the south transept and the fabric of the wall of the north are clues to the transeptal form of a twelfth-century church without aisles, but the general impression is of an almost complete rebuilding of the fifteenth century, datable more precisely by the south porch begun c. 1428 with a storey added seventy years later.

Kenneth Wickham remarked on the small size of the chancel in comparison with the lavish nave, 'unworthy ... of the great Abbey across the road' which could have provided funds more generously. The loss of the abbey was obviously not the reason why building stopped at Glastonbury as elsewhere; rather it was that religion as by law established under the Elizabethan Settlement hardly encouraged personal generosity towards church maintenance. Indeed, from that time onwards there is, in general, confrontation and the emergence of dissent. Yet Glastonbury in one sad event provides the first glimmer of toleration emerging through personal charity.

The town during the Civil War and afterwards was a divided community. Presbyterians and puritans had dominated both parishes, but many people remained quietly royalist and after the Restoration the Dyers were able to record in a brass monument in the chancel that Captain John Dyer for one had been entirely loyal to the king. But there were many dissenters in the town in the 1670s – Presbyterians, Baptists and Quakers – and when the duke of Monmouth's rebel army left Taunton on 21 June 1685 their planned route for Bristol led them first to Bridgwater and then to Glastonbury. Many found better shelter from the rain in the town's two churches than around bonfires in the roofless abbey. From among the townsmen at least 29 joined the duke.

The trials and savage sentences meted out to so many by Judge Jeffreys and his fellows

Glastonbury: *St John's church exterior*

Thomas Ken, 1667

especially at assizes in Wells and Taunton found men condemned to death or transportation herded in Wells into St Cuthbert's and the cathedral cloisters as well as in the more normal prisons in Bridgwater and Taunton. Among them in those days between sentence and execution moved the little man who had been bishop of the diocese for less than a year. Thomas Ken's first intervention saved a hundred men from summary judgement under martial law as the king's victorious army returned from Sedgemoor to London – men sated with victory and incited by a sermon preached by his predecessor Peter Mews on the theme of a subject's duty to his king. Peter Mews had been a royalist officer during the Civil War, the epitome of the Church Militant. Thomas Ken, as he was to prove, needed no lessons in duty to his king and he was later to record:

> It is well known to the diocese that I visited them
> [the prisoners] day and night, and I thank God I
> supplied them with necessaries myself as far as I
> could, and encouraged others to do the same.

It is evident that Ken visited prisoners in Taunton, for the churchwardens of St Mary's rang in October 'when the Bishop was in towne'. Either in Wells or in Glastonbury he more than once visited a particular rebel named John Hicks, a dissenting minister from Portsmouth who had joined Monmouth at Shepton Mallet. Hicks was condemned to die at Glastonbury and Ken, as he later wrote to Hicks's brother George, the respectable dean of Worcester, had several times 'visited ... and discourst long with him' and also sent his chaplain with Hicks to the scaffold.

During their discussions Ken exhorted Hicks

> to begge of God forgiveness for ye errours of his
> understanding, and for the sinnes those errours
> might occasion ... I pray'd with him [Ken went on]
> and repeated ye confession, and recommended him to
> ye Mercy of God, and he kneeled down & joyned
> heartily with us, & I hope God may be mercifull to him.

These are the words of a remarkable man who had gone so far as to offer this rebel dissenting minister his last communion. Hicks's own brother refused to plead for him on

123

account of his political and religious opinions. Ken the pastor saw beyond them, whatever his own views might have been, and Ken's last care for Hicks was to ensure for him a seemly burial to honour a minister of religion of good family. St John's church burial register contains the entry:

> John Hickes of Portsmouth in the county of
> Hampshire was buried in the Chancell of St
> John's Church in Glaston, October the 7th 1685.

Four years later Thomas Ken, loyal supporter of the divine authority of the Crown, found himself unable to agree to James II's Declaration of Tolerance and later unwilling to take the oath of allegiance to William III and Mary II after James's overthrow. Ken had shown his views of Toleration, but the king's Declaration was an attempt to override the authority of parliament. The oath of allegiance once made, believed Ken, could not be unmade. For his first offence he was imprisoned in the Tower of London, one of the famous Seven Bishops. For his second he was forced to leave his diocese and live in exile. He was not alone, and one of the other leading Non-jurors, as they were called, was George Hicks.

From his home at Longleat, just outside his former diocese, Ken must have been keenly interested in the work of the clergy he had come to know and the bishop who had so uncomfortably succeeded him. While Ken lived in a suite of rooms on the second floor of Lord Weymouth's mansion, surrounded by his library, the rather inept Richard Kidder, accepting the see under pressure, found himself struggling with recalcitrant clergy and awkward neighbours. The struggle was ended abruptly during the night of 29 November 1703 when both the bishop and his wife were crushed beneath one of the chimneys of the palace in Wells, which collapsed in a raging tempest. In the great storm which killed Kidder, Ken but barely escaped with his life. In this was a good deal of irony, since in the spring of 1702 Kidder had agreed with Queen Anne's suggestion that he should move to the vacant bishopric of Carlisle so that Ken, now that James II was dead, might return to Wells. Ken felt he was too old to move again. On Kidder's death the queen did not at first repeat her suggestion but her nominee George Hooper, an old friend of Ken, induced her to do so. Ken again refused, for parliament demanded an Oath of Abjuration about which he was unhappy, and he was now elderly and infirm. Besides, he declared, he had great faith in Hooper's ability to 'do excellent service to this sinking Church'.

Ken remained in retirement until his death in 1711 and lies buried, as he wished, just outside the parish church of St John, Frome, the nearest church in his old diocese; and, as he declared in his will, 'in the Holy Catholick and Apostolick Faith, professed by the whole Church, before the disunion of East and West; more particularly ... in the Communion of the Church of England, as it stands distinguished from all Papall and Puritan Innovations, and as it adheres to the doctrine of the Cross'.

E.H. Plumptre, *The Life of Thomas Ken*; R.W. Dunning, *Glastonbury, History and Guide*; A.K. Wickham, *Churches of Somerset*, 35.

Exalted to the Dignity of History
OARE, *St Mary*

~~≈∗≈~~

Charles Chadwyck Healey, lawyer and antiquarian, chose his words with care when he wrote his history of the parish of Oare. He quoted the reminiscences of the Revd W. H. Thornton who in the 1840s knew personally a number of Exmoor sheep stealers, poachers and smugglers, descendants in spirit if not in blood of a Monmouth rebel who escaped the notice of Judge Jeffreys after Sedgemoor for a dubious kingdom of his own. 'How many of the many readers of *Lorna Doone*,' he asked, 'bring themselves seriously to doubt whether Sir Ensor Doone and his family of ruffians ever existed in fact, or something nearly approaching to fact?' The recent arrival of a bronze statue in Dulverton is witness to the continuing popularity of Blackmore's story, or at least of Blackmore's heroine, both in Britain and the USA.

If Lorna still lives, then so does the drama which attended her wedding at Oare on that Whit Tuesday. Parson Bowden agreed to perform the ceremony, the parish clerk demanded a shilling fee for the parson from all men attending and double from all women. The churchwarden, who also happened to be the bridegroom, might protest, but since he always obeyed the parson he let the matter go. The little church was filled with Snowes and Ridds and even a Huckaback, and the bride sat at first in a pew half way down the nave before joining John Ridd at the altar steps. As soon as the marriage vows were made, a shot rang out and the bride fell. As the distrait bridegroom rode out to Black Barrow Down to seek revenge on Carver Doone who had fired the shot, Lorna was carried home on the pulpit door, her head resting on the pulpit cushion. Oare church had become famous.

R. D. Blackmore

There was, in history, no Parson Bowden at Oare in the reign of James II (when the story was set), but instead Elias Falvey, appointed in 1673 on the presentation of the merchant John Quicke of Minehead. Blackmore ought to have given a detailed description of the church: his father, after all, held the living between 1809 and 1842 and it is unlikely that it would have changed greatly from Falvey's day; but his father spent little time there and the author himself was brought up in South Wales, so perhaps historical information can hardly be expected. The parish's own records are few, the earliest a parchment register recording baptisms from 1674, marriages from 1675 and burials from 1691.

But there was a church at Oare by 1318, and no doubt long before. In that year William de Lynton acquired it by exchange for his vicarage of Christow and three months later went off on pilgrimage to Avignon with orders to return by the following Christmas. Few were the parishioners prominent and prosperous enough to leave a will until the sixteenth century, and not so many then but including two Warmans, a Rawle and a Redler. A century on and five Rawles paid tax in 1641 as well as John Blackmore in a list signed by the parson, a churchwarden and two overseers of the poor. The same tax was paid by a Richard Dune in Culbone and a Hugh Doone in Luxborough, hardly the sort of action one of Blackmore's villains would have contemplated. But no Ridd is mentioned at all.

Spurriers, Tapscotts, Rendalls, Broomhams and Rawles had children baptised at the font in the 1670s and 1680s. Parson Falvey baptised his own son William in 1688 and John,

Oare: *exterior*

Oare: *interior*

son of Christopher and Agnes Blackmore, was named in July 1699. Another Blackmore married a Rendall in 1681, Elizabeth Snow was successfully courted by John Rendall of Countisbury and Rawles, Passmores, Abbells, Tudballs and Spurriers went to church to be married. But no Doone is recorded as marrying a Ridd. How come, then, that a 'long gun' was preserved at Yenworthy Farm which, it was averred, had 'shot a Doone' ? Such folk were, of course, not likely to get involved with taxes and parsons' fees. This is the wild country of Exmoor.

The little church reveals so little of its history, for it is built of intractable stone far from quarries where a mason might exercise his art to produce a window or a door surround which an antiquarian could put a date to. When it was last rebuilt its records do not tell. Neither do the records of the diocese know much about the parish. Even during the careful enquiry into Protestant practice in 1554 no information came from Oare, and nothing again in 1557. At Archbishop Laud's visitation in 1634 the wardens were, as usual, silent, but their silence was this time noted. They were summoned to Wells and were forced to admit that the parish clerk, actually the son of the minister, had not been properly appointed although he had been doing the job for some years. They were also rather shamefaced about the state of the church floor; they did not report its poor state because they thought to anticipate trouble by ordering its repair. Unfortunately the work was not done. Two centuries and more later the outside world was just visible: in 1896 the parish obtained from the bishop a faculty to introduce not only a handsome new altar cloth but also a new American organ. The second was not a success so, by permission, it was removed in 1918 and replaced by the instrument which is still in use.

The outside world became yet more apparent during two world wars, and when in 1940 the threat of enemy invasion loomed worse than anything the Doones might have been thought to have done, the rector of Oare with Culbone was the first in the queue at Dulverton police station to offer his services. The Revd Creswell Webb, himself a former sergeant major in the Pioneer Corps in the First World War, was among a thousand men who in 24 hours signed up to defend Exmoor and west Somerset, their principal strength their fleet ponies and sturdy bicycles. In the event the invading Germans proved almost as ephemeral as the Doones, but not all on Exmoor is of the imagination. The Hallidays of Glenthorne are real and have been associated with the church since the mid nineteenth century. One of them, Ursula, played that organ for nearly twenty years until her death in 1992 and she and her husband Ben are remembered 'wearing gumboots and carrying a variety of implements' after making running repairs to the church tower. The church was built through such community spirit, and so it will survive.

R.D. Blackmore, *Lorna Doone*; C.E.H. Chadwyck Healey, *The History of the part of West Somerset comprising the parishes of Luccombe, Selworthy, Stoke Pero, Porlock, Culbone and Oare; Register of John Drokensford* (S.R.S. i), 11, 14; Somerset Protestation Returns; S.R.O. D/D/Ca 299; *Proc. Som. Arch.* Soc. cxxxv. 253; J. Hurley, *Exmoor in Wartime*, 1939–45, 34–5.

Parson Woodforde's First Cure
THURLUXTON, *St Giles*

~~❧~~

One of the many curates who served this church is better known than the rest not because of any deep religious conviction or pastoral zeal but because he kept a diary which, by surviving, has become famous. He left hardly a trace on this, his first cure, not out of neglect according to the standards of the day, but simply because he was there for a mere three months and actually resident for fifty-nine days.

It is not clear from the diary when James Woodforde decided to become a clergyman – probably it was something tacitly understood between himself and his father, who held the livings of Ansford and Castle Cary. As a member of New College, Oxford, from 1758 James consumed with his fellow students quantities of port, ran up tailors' bills, missed college prayers, played cricket, visited Oxford gaol and heard the occasional lecture. When at home in the vacations he went bear baiting or hare coursing and read the newspapers in the local inn.

Back at Oxford in his final year he was given a large work on moral philosopy to study for his examinations and met two Methodists. In April 1762 he had evidently decided on ordination and began studying the Epistles from the Greek Testament. Having thus resolved he took life rather more seriously, spending a whole June day at home in a tent in the garden over his Greek and refusing an invitation from a farmer to a sheep shearing feast on the grounds that to spend the evening before the Sabbath on such frivolities would be 'very improper'.

James Woodforde

After a year of such academic study he presented himself to the bishop of Oxford's chaplain at Christchurch for examination for deacon's orders. He spent half an hour construing part of Romans V and answered 'a good many hard and deep questions', after which he felt he had come off 'very well'. Four days later, in the presence of the bishop, he subscribed to the Thirty-Nine Articles of Religion and paid his fees. On the following day he was made deacon in a three-hour ceremony in Oxford cathedral. He took his degree three days later and soon began his clerical career by taking services at Newton Purcell, twenty miles from Oxford, in place of the incumbent who was too busy serving as one of the university proctors.

Woodforde preached his first sermon at Newton on a Sunday morning to fewer than 30 people and read prayers again in the afternoon, arriving back at Oxford at eight o'clock, the first of many Sunday excursions in the next few months. But in prospect was something further away and, if not permanent, at least a parish of his own. He had already received the offer, the curacy of Thurloxton, even before he was ordained.

Woodforde came to his little Quantock parish in October 1763 and lodged with Squire Cross for 1s 1 ½d a day, the price to include laundry and stabling for his horse. During that time he often rode back home to Ansford, and he spent a week in Oxford at the election of a new warden for Winchester College. By the end of November he had arranged to take the curacy of Babcary instead, but meanwhile, as he recorded in his diary, he and Squire Cross successfully coursed a hare one morning before breakfast and, on a typical Sunday, read prayers and preached in the morning, read prayers in the afternoon and, in addition, privately baptised the Squire's newest child. Otherwise he

Thurloxton: *exterior*

was the Squire's guest, dining and drinking with neighbours. On his last day he paid Mr Cross for his lodging and rode away on his horse named Cream with a cooked sheep's heart in his pocket for his first supper at Babcary.

The little red sandstone church still contains many features that Woodforde would have seen, though the building was much increased in size in the 1850s and again in 1868 by the addition of a vestry and of the north aisle. The plain font of c. 1100 perhaps marks the first sign of independence from the church's original foundation as a chapel within North Petherton's minster parish. The south wall of nave and chancel, and perhaps even the tower, mark a rebuilding in the twelfth century, judging by their proportions. The chancel was enlarged in the thirteenth century and in the fourteenth the east window was inserted, the font cover made and the tower remodelled. The west doorway was made in 1500, the porch added in the late sixteenth or the seventeenth century. Woodforde would surely have remembered the screen and pulpit, built in 1634 perhaps in anticipation of the demands Archbishop Laud was to make at his forthcoming visitation. It proved not enough, for three years later the rector and wardens declared that they had put up tables of the Ten Commandments and the Sentences, and had bought a 'flagon pot' as the archbishop's officers had required. Only a few years before Woodforde came to the parish the screen had been repainted with the name of the then churchwarden obliterating that of his 1634 predecessor. Both names can be seen only when the light shines at a particular angle.

J. Woodforde, *The Diary of a Country Parson*, selected by J. Beresford; *V.C.H. Somerset* vi. 321–2; S.R.O. D/D/Ca 299.

High Fashion in the Country
WOOLLEY, *All Saints*

A cupola is visible from across the valley on the road from Swainswick, just north of Bath, but the trees surrounding the churchyard almost hide the building from view at the bottom of Main Street. In style the church has been described as a 'country edition' of St James's in Bath, but the comparison can now only be made on paper since the city church was gutted in the raids of 1942 and demolished a decade or so later. The designer of this 'country church' was the sophisticated John Wood the Younger ('not an effort much to his credit' says Pevsner), a Yorkshireman whose contribution to Bath's splendour is so distinguished.

The classical style was *à la mode* in Bath when Wood was commissioned to replace the dilapidated ancient chapel of Woolley. It was *à la mode*, too, for the formal, restrained churchmanship of its time: a simple rectangular nave filled with plain box pews (the present ones came from a Bath city church in 1903), a small polygonal apse and, making a point in the landscape, a pretty domed west tower; just what the lady of the manor required.

That lady was Elizabeth Parkins, of Ravenfield in Yorkshire in 1761 but lady of the manors of Woolley and Charlcombe which she had inherited from her uncle William Parkins. Her generosity was recorded in the parish register at the time but was made public in the 1870s when workmen found a piece of parchment behind the skirting near the pulpit which declared that she had ordered what had become a dilapidated medieval chapel to be replaced at her sole expense. Thus could a landowner dispose.

Elizabeth had already in 1757 given the church a silver communion set together with a surplice, a Bible and altar linen. That gift, too, was recorded in the parish register, evidently neither by the minister nor the parish clerk but by Matthew Worgan, Mistress Parkins's steward and her eventual heir. Matthew himself was buried in the church in 1794.

The history of Woolley can, of course, be traced back much further. It was mentioned in Domesday Book, one of the many estates of the bishop of Coutances which, for some unknown reason, had then recently been linked with the bishop's manor of Bathwick. With Bathwick it remained for centuries and thus passed into the ownership of the nuns of Wherwell in Hampshire. When in 1321 a vicar was appointed for Bathwick, it was his responsibility to see that services were also held regularly at Woolley. In return the people at Woolley paid him the tithe of their garden produce, fees for particular services, and offerings in cash or kind according to custom. Woolley continued under Bathwick's

Woolley: *exterior*

vicars long after the dissolution of Wherwell; in fact the link was only severed in 1975 when three parishes in the valley, Woolley, Swainswick and Langridge, were placed under one rector.

A year later the 21 families of the parish were faced with a challenge: repair or redundancy. They chose repair, and a plaque inside the church declares their success. Aided by 'many friends', they found the money; and the more official Friends of Woolley Church, sponsoring a winter concert and a summer Strawberry Tea – far more than just a tea and in 1993 including a performance by the Northgate Rappers – continue to keep the church as it should be.

Church and churchyard hold the remains of many who sought a resting place in this delectable spot rather than among the popular bustle of Bath. Inside are tablets recording Mrs Charity Wiltshire, wife of one of the city's mayors whose business was to run carriages to London; and Thomas King, formerly of Walcot, whose skill as a monumental mason is displayed in churches well beyond Bath and who died in 1804 'with exemplary fortitude and resignation'. And under the churchyard trees lie, among others, Peter Grigg, rector of the parish for fifty-five years until his death in 1804; and Rear Admiral Peter Puget, whose name was given to the Sound off the north-west coast of the United States where he sailed under the command of Admiral Vancouver.

The parish registers tell of others who found the remoteness of Woolley an important part of its charm, for here they found a sympathetic parson prepared discreetly to celebrate weddings where prying eyes and parental objections might be avoided. Today's visitors will surely be noticed in such a small place, and warmly welcomed.

A. C-C, *All Saints Church, Woolley, Restoration Appeal* (1976); *Register of John Drokensford* (S.R.S. i), 179–80; *The Church Rambler* ii. 73–81.

Plain Exterior
FROME, *Wesley Church*

✦

When John Wesley first visited and preached at Frome in March 1753 he remembered it as 'a dry, barren, uncomfortable place'. For a century an important centre of the West-Country clothing industry, Frome had been a hotbed of nonconformity, 'such a mixture of men of all opinions, Anabaptists, Quakers, Presbyterians, Arians, Antinomians, Moravians and what not', Wesley recorded on a visit in 1768. Cobbett later described it as 'a sort of little Manchester'.

The story of Frome's Methodism, published by Stephen Tuck in 1837 at the request of the Wesleyan Quarterly Meeting and at the desire of the Chapel Committee, began some years before John Wesley's first visit after a pedlar from Bristol came to the town singing hymns. One of Mr Wesley's preachers followed him in 1746 or 1747 and preached in an orchard behind the Pack Horse inn.

Frome: *Wesley Methodist church exterior*

Established nonconformists in the town were 'straitened and fettered by High Calvinism or Arianism', Wesley was later to remark, and the Anglican response was naturally hostile, so preachers received a rough reception. Yet a small group of worshippers met together in Milk Street in a house formerly used by Baptists.

The meeting was unlicensed and the Anglican vicar, who was also a justice of the peace, employed some tough characters to create a disturbance. The vicar himself appeared and on the pretext that his shirt was torn had three women, including the householder Sarah Seagram, taken into custody. Sarah agreed before trial at Taunton to compound for a fine of £20 but, unable to pay, had her few possessions confiscated and herself thrown on the streets with her children. The little group was not without its supporters and their case was widely publicised in 1751–2. Probably in 1752 Charles Wesley preached in the town.

Before 1757 the cause was revived by seven people at a house in Broadway under the leadership of William Edington. Soon they were joined by six more including the three women so badly treated. The earliest membership list reflected the attraction of Methodism: nearly half were drawn from labourers in the clothing trade and others from the lower orders. In 1757 the group formed part of what was called the Wiltshire Circuit, whose largest congregation was at Coleford in the Mendips (174 members) and which stretched as far as Basingstoke and the Isle of Wight.

Frome: *Wesley Methodist church interior*

John Wesley

By 1761 the Frome society, still suffering a good deal from persecution, had 74 members, but such apparent success did not entirely satisfy Wesley: 'how zealous to hear are these people', he wrote on a visit in 1763, 'and yet how little do they profit by hearing'. In 1767 membership was a little smaller but when Wesley came that September the house he was to preach in proved 'too small, so many were constrained to go away'. Next evening he preached in a meadow 'where a multitude of all denominations attended ... God is at length giving a more general call to this town also.'

Membership of many Methodist societies in the county fluctuated and several came to an end in the later 1770s and 1780s. Frome's society prospered and a larger house was in use for meetings about 1770. It was not large enough to accommodate the crowd Wesley attracted on his visit in 1776, so he used a nearby meadow. In 1779 a larger building was opened at Keyford, on the site of the present chapel, but it was for long a financial burden on a membership of poor folk, a situation not helped by the insolvency of the treasurer. A Sunday school was opened in 1792 to teach poor children to read the Scriptures, but hired teachers proved unsatisfactory and for fifteen years and more the members struggled against debt and continued opposition. And they remained, as Wesley himself had done, still members of the Anglican Church until, in 1809, their minister gave Holy Communion to about 200 people. This act seems to have been the signal for a revival through the preaching of Edward Griffith, a local man. Frome's Methodist society doubled in size and nine new classes were formed to enable members to teach and support each other in the Wesleyan way.

In the face of this enlargement the chapel, only thirty years old, proved too small. It was therefore demolished and rebuilt on the same site, and was opened in May 1812. Perhaps rightly ignored by Pevsner, its plain exterior and elevated site makes it more citadel than place of worship, though the interior, with galleries on all sides and an impressive organ, is much more welcoming.

Collections and gifts towards the new building raised £1448, but that was rather less than the cost of a lawsuit between the chapel committee and the contractor, far less than the actual cost of the building itself, which was £2928. Further costs were added in 1816–17 when the children's gallery was lowered, the pulpit removed, a large vestry destroyed to make room for a communion table, and a building for the Sunday school was added. The society could not afford to pay all the interest on the debt, which in 1826 stood at £2900 and in 1836 at £2566. Nearly half was paid off as a result of a generous grant from the central Methodist General Chapel Fund and gifts from Thomas Fussell of Mells and others, so Stephen Tuck could claim in his history of the cause in 1837 that their prospects were 'once more of a bright and cheering description'.

For meanwhile in 1812 Frome had become the head of a new circuit; in 1813 the Sunday school had 260 children on its books, rather more boys than girls. In 1834 the chapel membership stood at 215, with 690 in the circuit; and in 1837 the total reached 390 with 1097 in the circuit. By 1837 Methodism had suffered division as well as multiplication in the formation of the Methodist New Connexion, Primitive Methodists and Bible Christians. By 1909 Frome's Methodists could worship either with the Wesleyans in Christchurch Street West or at the Mission in the Butts; with the Primitive Methodists in Sun Street, opened in 1834; at the United Methodist Free Church formerly in Catherine Street from 1851 and now at Portway; or at Bethel on Butts Hill, one of the chapels of the Wesleyan Reform Union, opened in 1858. The original Wesleyans, always the more prosperous, had a day school (founded in 1863) with 323 pupils. The Baptists and Congregationalists each had two chapels in the town.

In 1931, a year before the union of most of the Methodist branches, the Primitives at Sun Street, the United Methodists at Portway, and the Wesleyans still with their Mission supported four full-time ministers, but by 1939 Portway had become part of the Wesleyan circuit and the three chapels had two ministers between them. Sun Street remained part of a separate circuit until the 1960s; the Methodist union of 1932 was a long time coming.

Cuzner's Hand-Book to Froome-Selwood; S. Tuck, *Wesleyan Methodism in Frome;* P. Belham, *The Making of Frome.*

The Profanation of Ringers
EAST COKER, *St Michael*

The tower peeping through the trees surrounding Coker Court is a surprise, not because it reveals a church so close to the manor house, but because the style is not of Somerset at all. Pevsner was obviously puzzled by it, noting the arcaded parapet and window tracery which he dated to the early nineteenth century, but believing that it occupied the north transept thought it must predate the late Middle Ages. John Batten dated it (almost correctly) to 1791, a rather unlikely period for church building unless some disaster threatened. Recent research has concentrated on a much earlier period in another part of the building and has revealed a fascinating story.

Brian and Moira Gittos have discovered within the shell of the present nave the walls of a Saxon church. It can be seen, now they have pointed it out, above the thirteenth-century south arcade and in the west wall of the nave, its tall, narrow profile typical of Saxon churches like St Laurence's at Bradford on Avon; just the sort of church once to be found at Chilton Trinity or Wilton.

The arcade which pierced the south wall of that first building is evidence of enlargement in the thirteenth century – circular piers, moulded capitals and double-chamfered arches. Probably at that date the church had already been extended eastwards and had a central tower with shallow transepts. In the later Middle Ages a north aisle was added and the whole building was given new windows. Some of these enabled the Courtenays, lords of the manor, to display the heraldry in which most the their kind rejoiced. Here still survive, in the south transept which was probably their private chapel, the blue lion of Redvers, the greyhounds of Gaynesford, the emblems of Carminow and Arundel and, of course, the torteaux of Courtenay, tracing the family and its connections from the thirteenth to the early sixteenth centuries.

Hugh Courtenay, first earl of Devon, acquired the manor, and soon afterwards the advowson (the right to appoint rectors) about 1310. Trustees of the second earl in 1377 gave the advowson and the rector's endowment to help found a family chantry in Exeter cathedral. In place of the rector, a vicar was appointed with a much smaller income. To this day the vicars of East Coker are appointed by the dean and chapter of Exeter.

From 1385, incidentally, the vicars were assigned most of the former rectory house, grazing in the churchyard, a small meadow and a bed of alders, the right to let their pigs feed in the lord's woods and firewood from those woods including a Yule log. From their parishioners they were to receive the tithe of hay and garden produce, together with offerings in church. The dean and chapter of Exeter agreed to pay them a pension of 60s,

East Coker: *tower*

but in return they had to pay for all repairs to the chancel of the church, all taxes and other charges, and even had to offer hospitality to any of the canons of Exeter who came to visit.

Two small medallions in the window of the south transept have the arms of Helyar and Cary, two more Devon families. Both William Helyar, archdeacon of Barnstaple (and thus a canon of Exeter), and his son Henry married into the Cary family, and son succeeded father as lord of the manor of East Coker in 1645. Helyars occupied the family pew perhaps more frequently than the Courtenays before them for the Court was their principal home. Lady Joanna, wife of one of the many William Helyars, left £50 to beautify the building, but the family could not bring itself to part with the money until the central tower evidently threatened to collapse in her great-grandson's time. The parishioners described it as 'ruinous' when, unusually for the time, they applied to the bishop's chancellor in May 1791 for a faculty to build a new tower in place of that 'built upon arches which connect the chancel with the church'. They added that the tower, dividing chancel from nave, 'exposes the House of God to the profanation of Ringers upon all publick occasions'. The chancellor's fee was the huge sum of £4 19s 10d and postage came to 1s 1d.

The parish vestry at a meeting in June 1791 accepted the plans and estimates of Joseph Radford. Radford evidently undertook to build a new tower for the sum of £315, but the final cost of the work was to be more than twice that sum, partly because the design was several times modified, partly because the space left by the removal of the old tower had to be made good. The accounts of the wardens chart the progress of the work: removing the bells and lead from the old tower, digging up corpses for the foundation of the new one, 'keeping people out of church on Sundays whilst the church was open', making the new roof where the old tower used to be, buying reed and furze to protect the unfinished masonry from frost, a partition and some hessian to cover the altar piece (presumably the plaster affair which blocked the east window until 1857), coal and wood for a fire to air the church, and the sum of 4 guineas paid to Mr Williams for painting and gilding the dials of the clock.

Radford's plan was modified in many details. String courses and coping each increased by 3ins, walls were thickened, lights were added to windows, another foot to the height of the tower, 6ins to the height between cornice and balustrades. Oak rather than elm was used for the floor of the clock loft. The whole was a considerable undertaking and plastering was still being paid for well into 1793. Thanks to Mrs Helyar's £25, £50 from John Bullock, and a gift of £25 from the parish overseers there was cash in hand while the remainder was collected from parishioners by means of rates. The wardens' accounts do not suggest that there was any difficulty.

East Coker was prosperous enough in the late eighteenth century; a pretty village still, though much changed in the last twenty years through the proximity of Yeovil. The approach to the church passing Archdeacon Helyar's almshouses and facing the

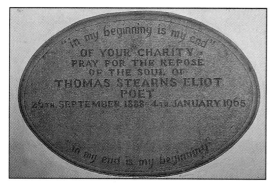

East Coker: *Eliot memorial*

East Coker: *glass in south transept*

medieval hall of Coker Court is essentially unchanged, pure English. The work of Joseph Radford has blended well. The scene appeals particularly to those visitors from opposite sides of the world for whom East Coker has fascination. For here, not far from the church, still stands the house where William Dampier was born in 1651; and elsewhere in the parish lived Nicholas Dodge and Andrew Elliott. Dampier sailed round the world three times and first described the coast of Australia. Dodge and Elliott found their way to New England, the one settling on the rocky Block Island, the other founding a clan which, when the new tower was almost a century old, produced Thomas Stearns Eliot. The narrow lanes which lead the visitors to East Coker from every direction led Eliot back to his roots, and it is here in the churchyard that his ashes have rested since his death in 1965.

J. Batten, *Historical and Topographical Collections; Proc. Som. Arch. Soc.* cxxxv. 107–11; C. Woodforde, *Stained Glass in Somerset 1250–1830*, 106–7, 220; S.R.O. D/D/C pet 1/95; ibid. D/P/cok. e 4/1/1.

A Comfortable Pew for His Lordship
HINTON ST GEORGE, *St George*

~~>◆<~~

Pouletts, originally from Pawlett, lorded it at Hinton from about 1430 until the death of the eighth and last Earl Poulett in 1973. They were lords of the manor, owners of most of the land, and from the later sixteenth century patrons of the living. They were, when it mattered, intensely loyal to the Crown but their rewards were modest: Sir Amias had been keeper of Mary, Queen of Scots, his grandson John was given a barony in 1627. There were heavy fines for the first baron and his heir for their support of the king in the Civil War; and an earlier Sir Amias is said to have suffered imprisonment at the hands of Cardinal Wolsey.

They saw themselves more impressive in death. Their parish church, of golden Ham stone, was begun in the early thirteenth century and was built long before Pouletts came to Hinton by masons who also worked at Wells cathedral. Pouletts and parishioners evidently financed a substantial rebuilding from the mid fifteenth century which included the west tower, begun in or about 1486, and the font, decorated with the Poulett arms. Probably at the end of the Middle Ages the north transept was transformed into a family chapel above a burial vault.

Hinton St George: *Poulett tombs*

The first Sir Amias Poulett was the first to be commemorated there after his death in 1538, his tomb one of an identical pair evidently built about 1540 by his son Sir Hugh, who did not occupy the second tomb chest until his death in 1572. Both chests, incidentally, had been used before. The recumbent figures, complete with kneeling children, are typical of their time, still Gothic in spirit, though the wall of each recess has foliage with a Renaissance flourish. The second Sir Amias died in London and was commemorated at St Martin's in the Fields – he who as the strict keeper of Mary, Queen of Scots, would not 'make so foul a shipwreck' of his conscience as to contrive a fatal accident. In 1728 the rebuilt St Martin's found, quite understandably, that it could do without his tomb, and

Hinton St George: *exterior*

the marble-painted plaster entablature now rises high above the tomb chest to dominate the chapel at Hinton. Beneath the chapel is a sealed vault where the remains of the commemorated still lie. When Lady Poulett died in 1653, a new brick vault was added to the west, and his lordship's accounts recorded the cost of velvet for the hearse and yards of black hangings, both in the church and across the churchyard in Hinton House.

So generations of Pouletts sleep with their fathers and generations worshipped (and perhaps even slept) not far away in the north aisle. They appointed the rectors, including one in Elizabeth's reign who was a member of the family, held two other parishes and lived in Jersey. Several achieved some notoriety. Edmund Peacham, rector from 1587, was in trouble in 1608 for uttering 'railing words' against the king. In 1614 he was put in the Tower of London for libelling Bishop Montague before the members of the High Commission, and he was sentenced to be deprived of his orders because his sermons and other writings roused suspicion. In 1615 he was found guilty of treason at Taunton Assizes and died in the following year in gaol there. Early in his time in the parish Peacham's successor, Richard Gove, fell out with one of his parishioners, who was sent to gaol until he submitted. About 1636 he also fell out with one of his churchwardens about who should have control of the church keys. Gove was from the beginning of his ministry sympathetic to the policy of Archbishop Laud and introduced frequent celebrations of the Holy Communion and installed an organ to improve the quality of worship.

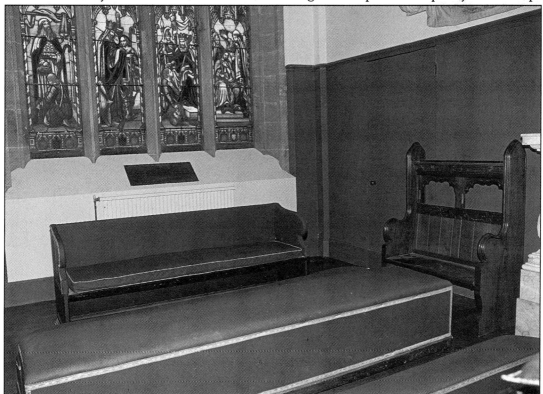

Hinton St George: *Poulett pew*

The second Baron Poulett welcomed the return of the king in 1660 and his grandson was elevated to an earldom for his loyalty to Queen Anne, whom he served as First Lord of the Treasury and Lord Steward of the Household. John Poulett, the fourth earl, was a military man who served during the Napoleonic Wars as Lord Lieutenant of Somerset, a key position in the defence of the realm.

Successive earls transformed Hinton House during the eighteenth century with the help of Matthew Brettingham and Sir John Soane. By 1801 James Wyatt was working there and his distinctive Gothic style is still in evidence. Wyatt was also commissioned to design a pew and mausoleum to form an extension of the family burial vault and to take the place of the former north aisle. An account book records the cost of removing stone from the churchyard in the summer of 1814, suggesting that the work may well have been overseen by Wyatt's nephew Jeffry Wyatville.

The mausoleum comprises a large brick room with shelving designed for the storage of 24 coffins. Still remarkably preserved, thanks to an impressive ventilation system, are 17 coffins including that of Rosa, Dowager Countess Poulett (died 1915), which is topped by an open coronet. Further east are three coffins, one of 1805 still covered with red velvet and decorated with upholstery pins and false hinges with gadrooning. Further east still, in the original vault but rearranged after the rebuilding, are at least 22 more coffins. All were examined minutely by an expert in the 1980s when it was feared (wrongly) that the dry rot found in the church could be attributed to decay within the vault.

The fine pew above the Wyatt vault was in a sense an extension of the house, and an inventory of the furniture drawn up in 1879 included comfortable chairs, upholstered kneeling desks, a carpet and fine bound Common Prayer books, a marked contrast to the bare chill of the rest of the church at the time. Memorials on the walls were a constant reminder of Poulett mortality, the latest by Peter McLennan of Bath commemorating George Amias Fitzwarrine Poulett, 8th Earl Poulett, who died childless in 1973, the last of his line, the last to use the splendid pew in which his ancestor hoped to demonstrate his superiority.

V.C.H. Somerset iv. 42–3, 48–50; S.R.O. DD/PT, boxes 48, 50; *Proc. Som. Arch. Soc.* cxxxii. 256–9.

An Antiquarian among Miners
CAMERTON, *St Peter*

✣

Camerton was the ideal parish for John Skinner. The fabric of its church, like that of most churches when he arrived in 1800, revealed history enough back to medieval times, but Skinner's taste was for more ancient things, for Roman roads and the artefacts of a prehistoric age. Choosing first to be a lawyer, he unfortunately retained the instinct to defend his own at all costs which made him a difficult neighbour. When instead he chose the Church, he read for Orders most assiduously with the aged rector of his native parish of Claverton. From the Revd Mr Graves it seems John Skinner acquired his love of antiquities and probably his mistrust of Methodists. His examination for priest's orders and his ordination took nearly five days out of a projected trip to prehistoric sites in Devon and Cornwall.

The parish of Camerton provided Skinner with a comfortable living, but he could never be comfortable when farmers practised tithe evasion, colliers exercised profligacy and the lord of the manor attempted to alter a boundary to the detriment of rectory land. But Skinner, who revealed all his problems to a voluminous journal later bequeathed to the nation, was of his time a caring pastor, concerned for regular and decent worship and the general spiritual care of his flock. He visited the sick whenever he was sent for, prepared sermons with the greatest care and was much disturbed at the lack of support he received from the lady of the manor over the village school. He certainly failed to understand the Methodists who were making such headway among his flock, but put his finger on the cause of their success and general Anglican failure by his observation that they might be of great help to clergymen if they would act like catechumens in the early Church 'as they know far better the private life and disposition of the poorer orders'.

The lack of proper Church education was serious: in 1823, as was his custom, Skinner held a series of catechism classes, but on examination he could only recommend one boy out of 14 for confirmation although he was happy with the answers of the 18 girls. The cause, he felt, was the lack of a school for boys. Those 15 Camerton children joined about 500 others at Frome for the confirmation service.

John Skinner was unusually sympathetic towards the Roman Catholics of the area and was fascinated by a native of his parish some years before his time. 'Dr' Coombes of Meadgate (inoculator, blacksmith, tooth-drawer and later beer seller) who, formerly a prominent singer in church ('having a good stentorian voice for psalmody'), fell out with the other singers, left the Church and sent both his son and his nephew to be educated at Douai. The son was priested on his return and opened a Catholic chapel in his house at Meadgate. Skinner attributed chapels at Shortwood and Shepton Mallet indirectly to

Camerton: *exterior*

Fr Coombes, and he was very tempted to attend the consecration of the monastery chapel at Downside in 1823, though in the event he declined and sent his brother instead for fear his parishioners should misunderstand.

The parishioners at Camerton were inclined to worship as the fancy took them. One woman who attended the Catholic chapel reported to him when she returned to the parish church that the Catholics were kind to the poor but 'she never got much good from their doctrines'. The Methodists proved another haven for discontented Anglicans, especially for the church singers. In fact Skinner was in 1822 very happy that they had gone for a time since he replaced them with girls from the school who were much more to his satisfaction than 'the great Bulls of Basan' who had previously occupied the gallery. Fewer than 20 people stayed to receive the Holy Communion after an unusually well attended Christmas morning service in 1827, much to the rector's disappointment.

Skinner was a man of huge archaeological appetite, keen to dig into every burial mound he could find for miles around but apt to imagine sites to be of greater significance than the evidence justified. Yet his observations proved of the greatest value to local archaeologists of the twentieth century, leading Abbot Horne, parish priest of St Benedict's, Stratton on the Fosse, and his pupil and collaborator William Wedlake to highly significant sites in Camerton and beyond.

Skinner himself realised that his church stood on such a site, but the extension of the churchyard in 1892 and more modern bulldozing has all but erased the earthworks which surrounded it on three sides. He thought it a 'British Meeting Place' or 'Place of Assembly', but it was probably Roman in origin and marks the site of the earliest settlement on a limestone terrace between the Roman Fosse Way and the Cam valley. That the church is at its centre leaves the important possibility that here is an early Christian site. The Saxon cemetery higher up the hill was clearly Christian by the seventh century.

Beyond that Skinner appears to have had little interest in the fabric of his church, though he did record and preserve several twelfth-century grave slabs found during the repaving of the chancel, together with an early fourteenth-century memorial to Elias Cotele, lord of the manor. The fine tower, with its grotesques and fascinating corbels including an elephant, a rhinceros, and human figures bearing a zither, beads and a cream skimmer, interested him not at all.

He was, however, concerned that the building by his time was not large enough for the growing population of the parish and had his own clear – and very sensible – ideas. The church then comprised a medieval nave and chancel and a north chancel chapel, built in 1638 by the Carew family, lords of the manor. There was also a north porch and a west tower, both still in place. Skinner's idea was to build an aisle on the north side of the nave and rebuild the porch further north as the main entrance. The young Mr John Jarrett, lord of the manor and patron of the living, did not find the plan appealing, for the new work would almost touch his manor house and would obstruct the private entrance to the chapel the Carews had built. A few years later Mr Jarrett built Camerton Court a hundred yards from the church, but did not change his mind about Skinner's extension.

The Revd Wilfrid Lawson Jarrett, who succeeded Skinner, saw his cousin's point of view and extended the church to the south instead, creating the necessary space but at the same time producing an architectural monstrosity. Beside the chancel he built a second chapel, and west of it a long, narrow aisle southwards with a gallery for girls above it. The old pews in the nave, a new gallery over the west end and another in the tower for boys provided a grand total of 500 seats, which of course included a spacious one for the Jarrett family between their chapel and the chancel and a 'family' pew by the font. The oddest feature was the arrangement of the reading desk and the pulpit, up steps opposite each other where the new aisle joined the nave. Perhaps that gave rise to the comment made by a visitor in the 1870s of the rivalry between the parson and the clerk:

> The Rector read the service, but his voice was
> eclipsed whenever the opportunity came by that of
> a peculiarly noisy clerk who ... figuratively speaking
> bore down all before him ... It was in the Litany that
> the clerk specially distinguished himself ... His
> accent is impossible to describe, his inflexions of
> voice may be graphically represented thus – 'Goo' Lor'
> deliver US' it being understood thereby that the verb
> was almost inaudible, because the voice was gathering
> itself up to eject the last syllable with thunderous power.

The plan of the alterations was as nothing compared to the decoration of the interior. The walls were thickly ochred, the roof timbers largely hidden by coved plaster ceilings; fixed around the walls was 'the range of hat-pegs which argues such want of respect for the house of God'. And such a building, on one Sunday chosen at random by a visitor in 1876, attracted beyond the school children and the choir not more than thirty people.

A few years on and Jarretts put right what their family had so damaged. The Misses Anna Mary and Emily Elizabeth Jarrett, only children of John Jarrett, undertook an extensive rebuilding and restoration in 1891–2, converting (as Miss Emily Jarrett declared in a pamphlet recording the work) something 'most unsightly and inconvenient' to 'some sort of ecclesiastical propriety'. The work involved the creation of a new chancel, thus lengthening the nave, and a new south aisle extending eastwards beyond the new chancel screen and an organ chamber and single storey vestries along the south side.

Few original features survive, for the old nave roof was found to be rotten and the south door too damaged to be retained, but it is clear that the nave and chancel were both in the Perpendicular style, although two arches found in the south wall at the restoration suggest something older. The rood stair door in situ just east of the north porch, also

Camerton: *carving on tower*

found at the restoration, shows the size of the original nave. Other survivals are the Jacobean font cover and the eighteenth-century pulpit.

The work of restoration was in the hands of the distinguished architect Thomas Garner of London and many of the fittings were supplied by leading ecclesiastical suppliers of the day like Messrs Bell of Bristol, Wippells of Exeter and Watts of London. The organ, by Vowles of Bristol, was the particular gift of Miss Anna Mary Jarrett. The whole cost not far short of £4000, the greater part of which was given by the two generous sisters. Mr Skinner would have felt himself entirely justified; his own chronic depression led to suicide and an unmarked grave.

Journal of a Somerset Rector (1822–32), edd. H. Coombs and A.N. Bax; *Journal of a Somerset Rector* (1803–34) edd. H. and P. Coombs; *Church Rambler;* E.E. J[arrett], *History of St Peter's Church, Camerton;* S.R.O. DD/SAS, Wedlake papers.

A Distinguished Scholar Priest
ISLE BREWERS, *All Saints*

~❦~

The little Victorian church in the valley of the river Isle serves a tiny community whose name fascinates visitors. The name Isle seems to defeat place-name experts, who can only link it with a Greek word which means water. Brewer is the name of a family which long ago owned the estate and specifically of William Brewer. He was a powerful man, a royal justice from the time of Henry II, a member of the council of regency when Richard I was abroad on Crusade, and a negotiator for his release. He was a loyal supporter of King John and remained influential under Henry III until his death in 1226.

Such a man of power was richly rewarded with estates (Bridgwater about 1199, Axminster 1201) and like many of his contemporaries he founded an abbey (Dunkeswell) and a hospital (St John's, Bridgwater), endowing each with land or other forms of income. By 1219 the new hospital was given the church of Isle as part of this act of piety – just possibly with a notion of spiritual insurance, too – which gave the hospital

Isle Brewers: *All Saints' church, 1841*

Dr Joseph Wolff

the right to present rectors to the living. In due course the hospital took a larger share of the church's income, probably the corn and other great tithes, leaving the parish in the care of a much less well paid vicar.

So this remote place hardly attracted men of great distinction, although one, Stephen Lyons, was excommunicated in 1554, probably for refusing to put away his wife. And it is quite probable that few if any of his parishioners knew how distinguished was the man who became their vicar in 1845. They remembered him for his kindness and affability, for his remarkable sermons preached in a loud voice; and a friend recalled his childlike innocence and his deep Christian faith.

That man was Joseph Wolff, born the son of a Jewish rabbi in what is now central Germany in 1795. Learning Latin and Greek as well as Hebrew at an early age and beginning to have doubts about the faith of his fathers he left home and at the age of seventeen received Christian baptism at a Catholic monastery near Prague. Supported at the university of Tubingen by a Viennese aristocrat he began to study eastern languages. He then travelled to Rome where he received help from Pope Pius VII and taught Hebrew to the man later to be Pope Pius IX. But the young man taxed the patience of his supporters and was escorted from Rome by a detachment of gendarmes.

He found refuge in a Swiss monastery for a time but later travelled to England where he found in the banker Henry Drummond a patron who paid for him to go to Cambridge. He renewed his study of oriental languages and was taught theology by Charles Simeon. During this time he became a member of the Church of England.

Still supported by Drummond, Wolff set out in 1821 on a five-year missionary journey which took him to the Jewish communities in Palestine, Egypt, the modern Iran and Iraq, the Crimea, Georgia and the then Ottoman Empire. On his return he married an earl's daughter (and great-great niece of Robert Walpole) and then was off again, at first to Jewish groups in the British Isles and the Mediterranean and then as far afield as the modern Afghanistan and India. On his way to Kabul he was robbed and chained with slaves and in Madras contracted cholera; in Lucknow he was given money by the king of Oudh and in Delhi was presented with a robe of honour by the Great Mogul.

In 1835 Wolff began a third journey which took him to Malta, Cairo and Sinai, Abyssinia and Bombay, and then westwards to America, where he was made deacon by the bishop of New Jersey and received the degree of Doctor of Divinity at Annapolis. In 1838 the bishop of Dromore ordained him priest and Trinity College, Dublin, made him a Doctor of Laws.

For a time he stayed in England, serving successively as curate of Linthwaite and High Hoyland in Yorkshire where he was very happy, but the call of the east proved too much and in 1843 he determined to go to Bokhara to find the two English explorers, Stoddart and Conolly. Styling himself the 'Grand Dervish of England, Scotland and Ireland and of the whole of Europe and America' he set off equipped with clerical and academic robes. The two explorers had already been executed before Wolff set out and in eighteen months on his own journey he was several times in extreme peril.

On his return in 1845 Wolff was presented to the vicarage of Isle Brewers and in a ministry of seventeen years there built a vicarage and school, paid part of the salary of the schoolmistress, and gave food and fuel to the poor. He was much in demand as a preacher, and it was through his fame as a traveller that he managed to raise funds for his projects.

'Churchgoer' was as fascinated by the man as were many other people, particularly for his style in the pulpit, where he would

> pour forth his heterogeneous mass of miscellaneous learning – multitudinous language, anecdote, personal adventure and rich orientalisms – which he curiously enough called a sermon ... Yet who ... ever heard a discourse which they listened to with such rivetted interest or from which ... they derived such amusement? ... How he tossed up his hands, in his excitement, as he told over again his 'moving accidents by flood and field' – how he wrought himself up into such a phrenzy of zealous fervour, until he shouted out as if bellowing to a camel driver in the desert. ... You see yourself how little of his company the poor people of Isle Brewers must have, while he is lecturing or preaching, or wandering about with his curious adventures from pulpit to platform; nor can his parishioners be quite sure that tomorrow he may not be off to Crim Tartary or Cochin Chine ...

The preaching and lecturing were to some purpose for his last great effort was to build a new church. The old building was remote from most of the houses in the parish and was often flooded in winter. A new site was offered by the patron, General Michel of Dewlish (Dorset), but the cost was substantial and ever since he had openly supported Archdeacon Denison in 1855 Wolff had been under suspicion for his High Church

Isle Brewers: *All Saints' church*

views. The leading men of the parish had evidently been encouraged to oppose him, but when they saw the advantages of his plan they surprised him by voting a rate without being asked.

That was in October 1858 when he was recovering from illness. Just before Christmas he wrote to the bishop outlining progress and assuring his lordship in a postscript that no one disliked the system of auricular confession more than he did. He also wrote to an official at Wells declaring that he had secured the sum of £767 (including £10 from Lord Fitzwilliam and £5 from Lord Malmesbury) and proposed to commence work when he had £1000 so long as a faculty could be granted for which he could not at the time raise the fee.

Archdeacon Denison was prepared to support 'poor old Woolff'and a faculty was swiftly granted in March 1859. C.E. Giles of London and Taunton provided plans both of the old church and of the new one, the old with seats for 126 people including a little western gallery, the new with a total of 181 including benches for 72 children at the back.

The new church was consecrated in August 1861 and the final cost was about £1300. The builder was Mr Spiller of Taunton, the tesselated pavement was the work of Mr Brinson of Curry Mallet and the chancel window was designed and given by Mrs Miles of Bingham Rectory, Nottingham. The old bells and the Royal Arms of 1660 were rehung in the new porch-tower. After the service of consecration the distinguished company, including High Churchmen such as Archdeacon Denison, Prebendary J. E. Lance of Buckland St Mary and J. S. Coles of Shepton Beauchamp, lunched in a tent at the Vicarage, while the singers and 'such as could obtain tickets from the vicar' ate in the schoolroom. In the afternoon Prebendary Lance preached a sermon 'principally of a condemnation of the Essays and Reviews'.

Lady Georgiana Wolff died in January 1859, and lies buried outside the east end of the church. Just over two years later Dr Wolff married Louisa King, sister of the M.P. for Herefordshire and sister-in-law of Archdeacon Garbett. Dr Wolff himself lived for less than a year after his marriage and was buried beside his first wife under the shadow of his church. He left a building of gleaming lias and Ham stone in a new churchyard. Now there are mature trees and an attractive nesting place for some of nature's greatest travellers. 'The swallows have returned. Please close this door,' runs a very practical notice.

H.P. Palmer, *Joseph Wolff; Taunton Courier*, 13 February, 7 August 1861; S.R.O. D/D/Cf 1859/2; ibid. D/D/B reg. 38; J. Coombs, *George Anthony Denison; The Churchgoer's Rural Rides* (3rd edn. 1851).

Without a Faculty
CHARLTON MUSGROVE, *St Stephen*

The tower is the most impressive part of the church – rectangular in plan and with a fine selection of gargoyles, grotesques, pinnacles and battlements. The main timbers of the nave and south porch, still retaining their original colour, and the panelled chancel arch indicate much rebuilding in the fifteenth century and the niche beside the chancel arch once had a painting of the patron saint of similar date. However, the proportions of the building suggest a twelfth-century origin, probably founded by the Rivers family before the Musgroves became lords of the manor in the thirteenth century and gave the place their name. From that first building survive the three grouped lancets in the chancel. Next to them is a two-light addition of the fourteenth century.

Pews, pulpit and choir stalls, as in so many churches, are plainly Victorian, and these are very odd indeed. So is the north wall of the nave, which varies in width and includes a

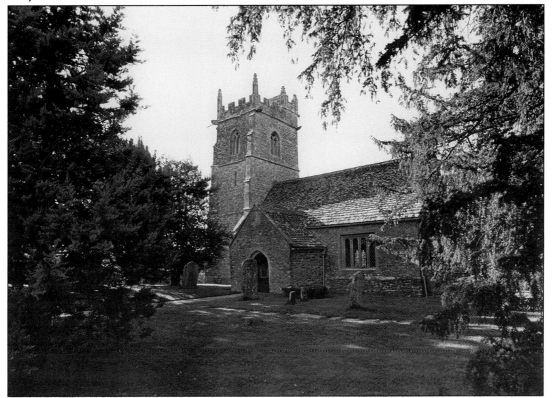

Charlton Musgrove: *exterior*

157

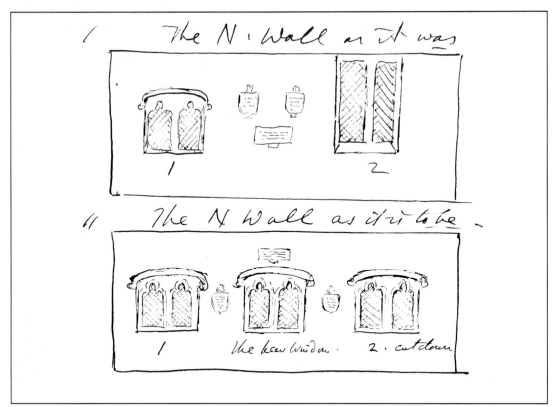

Charlton Musgrove: *C. E. Leir's restoration, 1884*

blocked north doorway and a chimney, both only visible from outside, and three windows, only apparently of the same design. All this was the work of the rector, Charles Edward Leir, in 1884. Such changes should, even in those remote days, have been undertaken only with the bishop's permission by means of a faculty, but Mr Leir regarded the church as something akin to his private chapel. After all, his family had been rectors, literally without a break, since 1617 and patrons of the living since 1661.

The bishop's registrar very politely demanded proper procedure: plans must be submitted to show proposed changes, followed by the publication of a citation, a formal legal notice to allow people to object to what was suggested. Mr Leir, in his rather auto-cratic way, had simply informed the registrar that he proposed to begin and when pressed sent a sketch of the north wall, explaining that he himself was constituted 'chief manager and overseer' of the work and had 'no plans but what are devised in my own head and carried out under my direction'. He added that he proposed to recolour and stencil the walls, add dossal hangings behind the communion table, and remove the west gallery. There was no mention of the removal of the pulpit, only a little over a century old, nor of the new pews and choir stalls.

Faced with such intransigence the registrar gave way, but he sent one of his staff from

Wells to Charlton to serve the citation in the proper manner and in due course issued the faculty. Mr Leir was not amused, for with the faculty came the inevitable bill, and among the items was one to cover the cost of the man sent with the citation. What particularly annoyed Mr Leir was that he had been sent on a day 'when he could not avail himself of the railway'.

In the sanctuary at Charlton are other tangible reminders of the rule of the Leirs: memorials of the first rector in the family, Richard Leir, appointed in 1617, who served without interruption until his death in 1654; and of his son Thomas, who continued his ministry in the days when the Church of England was temporarily in abeyance during the Interregnum and was properly instituted as rector only at the Restoration. Leir followed Leir as rector, with one exception, until the death of Lewis Randolph Marriott Leir in 1914, and the exception was Lewis Charles Davis, his brother-in-law. Leirs or their trustees followed each other as patrons until the death of Robert Beckett Marriott Leir in 1976.

The family, who had as much interest in Ditcheat as in Charlton, were landowners as well as rectors; squarsons, as the saying went, both squires and parsons, hunting and sitting on the Bench with their neighbours. Ever since 1661 they had been among the leading landowners in Charlton and the papers which found their way into the parish chest included the only surviving records of Charlton manor court and a fascinating glimpse of a Leir on tour in the form of a draft contract for the hire of camels in Egypt in 1847.

The Leir estate in Charlton and Wincanton, amounting to over 925 acres, was sold in 1920 after the tragic death of their owner; and tragedy still dogged their creation when in 1939 the fine rectory house built by Paul Leir in 1805 was destroyed by fire. Only the coach house remains. But St Stephen's, rather isolated on its little hill and virtually abandoned during the Second World War, is clearly well cared for and regularly attended.

V.C.H. Somerset vii (forthcoming); S.R.O. D/P/ch. mu and D/D/Cf.

High and Mighty
FROME, *St John the Baptist*

Frome's church has a recorded history dating back to a grant of Pope Sergius I which St Aldhelm obtained in the early 690s to ensure that his foundation above the River Frome should be 'free from all secular service'. Aldhelm's church was still recognisable in the late eleventh century, but by then it was no longer the home of a community of mission priests charged with spreading the Faith in middle Selwood but a parish church at the heart of a royal town; and, far from being free from the secular as Aldhelm had hoped, it was like Milborne Port in the hands of a grasping government official in Edward the Confessor's house-

The Revd W. J. E. Bennett

hold, a cleric named Regenbald, who recognised a prize when he saw one and managed to hold it long after the Conquest.

It is impossible to do more than guess at the physical appearance of Regenbald's church; any part which still survived in the nineteenth century was totally rebuilt between 1852 and 1866. Vicar W.J.E. Bennett noted what he called Saxon arcades at the western end of the nave, but Sir Stephen Glynne only remarked that the arcades were formed with piers without capitals. Fragments of Saxon carving built into the tower are the only certain remains, but not necessarily from Aldhelm's time, though at least one antiquarian has suggested that it is part of a cross erected to mark the progress of Aldhelm's cortege from Doulting in 709.

Bennett was not an antiquarian and did not pretend to be so, but he wrote a book entitled *The Old Church of St John of Froome* in which he described what he saw as the deficiencies of the building for the kind of worship which he was determined to introduce. He came to Frome in 1852 with a reputation – indeed, a petition was presented against his institution to the House of Commons – a reputation for enthusiasm for ritual which the prevailing fear of Roman Catholicism greatly magnified.

> You think, (not all, I hope, I am only addressing
> those who do) [he wrote in a pastoral letter to
> his new parishioners] that I ought to be a Roman

Catholic, and that I am more than half one in reality now. A very earnest lover of the Church of England I am; a very anxious and faithful abider by all the laws, customs, and images of the old Catholic Church of England, in opposition to the modern school of the last century, I am.

The church, for all its previous Protestant clutter, had much to commend it from Bennett's point of view. Frome clothiers of the Later Middle Ages had been prosperous and there were chapels north and south of the large chancel. In the 1540s there had been three chantries within the church, with altars to St Andrew, St Nicholas and Our Lady and a will made at the beginning of the sixteenth century mentioned lights of the High Cross, All Souls and All Saints. Such a building could become again a spiritual force in which restored liturgy would take pride of place.

Bennett's ability to preach both to rich and to poor and his utter sincerity convinced enough parishioners for him to take the first great step forward: within four years pews and galleries were removed, the pulpit was placed in a less prominent position on the north side of the chancel arch and open seats all faced eastwards towards the altar, the focal point of an ordered ritual. The cheerful abandonment of pew-privilege was worth celebrating and the leading Tractarians of the land came to celebrate, including Archdeacon Denison and E.B. Pusey. Keble was prevented by illness.

It was one thing to re-order the furniture and change the balance of worship. Another, equally fundamental, problem was the dangerous state of the fabric. Benjamin Ferrey had restored the chancel and St Andrew's chapel in the 1840s but these improvements only served to emphasise the dilapidation of the rest – 'a mere ruinous heap ... a crumbling mass ready to fall about our ears' as Bennett graphically wrote. So between 1860 and 1866 C.E. Giles was permitted effectively to rebuild the whole church with the full approval of the vicar, with little concern for the destruction of much that was of historical and antiquarian importance. 'It is "THE OLD CHURCH STILL",' Bennett declared, but only in spirit, not in reality.

The new building proved eminently suitable for Bennett's impressive restoration of ritual. The Church Rambler described in great detail the ceremony of a morning service he attended. In spite of his opinions against ritual and his disappointment that neither the vicar nor his sermon were as impressive as he had been led to believe, he nevertheless recorded the sermon in great detail and left his readers with the feeling that his prejudices had been shattered.

Bennett's concern for ordered and meaningful worship within the church was reflected in his parish organisation. It was divided into 12 districts, each with a visitor who was charged to have concern for rich and poor alike. A curate recalled that 'schools, classes, dispensary, provident clubs, soup kitchen, blankets and other charities, were all in

Frome: *St John's church, the Calvary*

Frome: *St John's church, Saxon fragments*

perfect working order', and vicar and curates visited regularly and taught daily in the schools. There was also a choir school for 12 boys, a home for factory girls, a crèche for babies whose mothers also worked in the town's factories. The classes included one for boys and girls after confirmation. And there was an educational publication, the precursor of the parish magazine, known as *The Old Church Porch*.

The rebuilding of the church and the employment of a succession of curates could not have been achieved without a private purse and the energy and generosity of many supporters, but Bennett early in his time at Frome made one startling change which won him the support of the many Dissenters in the town, namely the abolition of the compulsory church rate and the ending of pew rents. In their place he introduced what was then a remarkable innovation, that the congregation should support the work of the parish by their offerings in church, half of which should be for church expenses, a quarter for schools and a quarter for the poor.

Vicar Bennett died at Frome, still in office at the age of 82, if not beloved by all then highly respected. Accused at least once of heresy, he was the author of many books and one of the influential figures of the Tractarian movement. In the fifteenth century Edmund Leversedge, a member of a family for long resident in Frome, had an amazing other-worldly vision which, on recovery from his trance, he communicated to the three priests of Frome. Bennett's vision had more substance. It made him a pauper but he left his parish infinitely the richer for his ministry.

W.J.E. Bennett, *History of the Old Church of St John of Froome*; idem, *Pastoral Letter to the Parishioners of Frome*; F. Bennett, *The Story of W.J.E. Bennett*; M. McGarvie, *Light in Selwood; The Church Rambler* ii. 165–84.

Something Unique in the Diocese
HORNBLOTTON, *St Peter*

During the primary visitation of Bishop Gilbert Bourne in 1554 the churchwardens of Hornblotton complained that the 'sylyng' over the sacrament – by which they meant the chancel roof – and also the parsonage house were in 'great decay', a not unusual story at the time. The rector was to blame. By the 1870s the same could have been said again of the church although the parsonage house was then rather new, having been built by the then rector in 1867 to the designs of F.C. Penrose, surveyor of St Paul's cathedral. But the church was indeed ruinous, so ruinous that it was decided to begin again a few feet to the north of the old one, leaving just the west gable and the belfry. This time the rector, Godfrey Thring, and his wife between them took entire responsibility.

The Thrings were a talented and generous family who lived long and had a deep religious faith. The Revd John Gale Dalton Thring succeeded his father as owner of nearby Alford and patron of both Hornblotton and Alford in 1830. He lived to be nearly ninety

Prebendary Godfrey Thring

and was both squire and parson of Alford, taking his place on the Bench and as deputy lieutenant and at the same time serving as rector of Alford until handing over to his son Godfrey when he was well over seventy. Of his five sons, Theodore was a barrister and succeeded him as squire, Henry (later Baron Thring) was the first official parliamentary draughtsman, and Edward was the famous Headmaster of Uppingham School.

Godfrey, the fourth son, was educated at Shrewsbury and then Balliol college, Oxford (where his mother's brother was Master). He was ordained in 1846 and served as curate in four parishes in Berkshire and Norfolk over the next eleven years, interrupted by a period of ill health when he spent some time in the Middle East. One who met him there remembered fifty years later 'his culture, his many accomplishments ... the poetic grace of his mind ... and the piety of his heart'. In 1858 his father arranged for a private Act of Parliament by which the livings of Alford and Hornblotton were united, and in that same year Godfrey became rector. The income was handsome, over £535 a year including the glebe farm of over a hundred acres. For the next quarter of a century Godfrey ministered to the people of the two parishes, during that time publishing four volumes of hymns and other verses including the Church of England Hymn Book which went into three editions.

At the heart of his ministry was the parish church just behind his rectory at Hornblotton, and finding its fabric in such decay he commissioned a young London architect, Thomas Graham Jackson, to design an entirely new building. The corner stone was laid on 11 November 1872 by the rector's wife, and to mark the occasion the parishioners presented her with the silver trowel and mallet she had used. Fifteen months later, on an 'exceptionally fine' day in late February 1874, the bishop of the diocese came to consecrate the new building.

For the parishioners the day must have been memorable and it was recorded in great detail in the *Western Gazette* for 27 February. There were two services, morning and afternoon, the bishop's sermon was 'impressive', the principal inhabitants of both parishes were entertained at the rectory, and the poor were 'liberally supplied with tea and cake in the evening'. Offerings at the two services, amounting to over £15, were put towards a new bell.

Hornblotton: *exterior*

Hornblotton: *interior*

A piscina and memorial in the present vestry and the font are the sole survivors of the old church; all the rest was made new, the windows in a generally thirteenth-century style, most of the rest offering something unique in the diocese. Outside, the tile-hung belfry and broach spire and even the orange stone suggest Surrey or Sussex although the tiles were made in the parish and the stone for the walls was quarried at Hadspen and for the dressings at Doulting. Inside there are representations of Moses, Isaiah, Jeremiah and the Annunciation, texts from Scripture, and sprays of leaves and sunflowers all in strawberry red revealed by cutting away a covering layer of white plaster or cement, a process known as sgraffito and carried out here mostly by Francis Wormleighton with some by Owen Gibbons. Pulpit, choir stalls, lectern and vestry door are of oak with appropriate texts and native birds inlaid with satin wood, holly, ebony and black walnut by a process known as intarsia by W. E. Voss. The fine reredos includes Derbyshire alabaster by Thomas West of Hibbins and West with the figures of the four Evangelists painted on earthenware by William de Morgan. The mosaic pavement in the chancel was designed by Jackson and made by James Powell of the Whitefriars Glassworks in London and other encaustic tiles were by William Godwin of the Lugwardine Works. Powell also made the fine glass to Jackson's designs.

The artists were 'foreigners' but the workmanship was local: Messrs Clarke and Son of Bruton were the builders, and Charles Bentley was clerk of works. Mr Martin, churchwarden, and Messrs Green and Moody 'actively assisted' in the work, and the stone was hauled from the quarries by local farmers. The whole cost £2832 17s 9d of which the rector and his wife paid over £2500.

There was one more improvement to come, the electro-mechanical turret clock installed about 1883 by Charles Shepherd of London. It was the first electric clock in England with a striking apparatus, driven by batteries installed in the rectory well over a hundred yards away. Its face was turned towards the rectory, for none in the village could possibly see so far. A hundred years later the clock was removed to the Science Museum in London.

Thomas Jackson remembered Godfrey Thring as one of his best and most valued friends, and often stayed at the rectory. In 1876 Thring was made a prebendary of Wells and in 1893, at the age of seventy, he resigned the living. He died ten years later.

St Peter's church, generously open to those discriminating visitors who diligently follow the signs through the grasslands of the parish, is now joined with four other parishes as well as with Alford in the benefice known as the Six Pilgrims. Twenty-five people on the electoral roll represent nearly a third of the population of the parish who preserve the great gift made by Godfrey Thring.

S.R.O. D/P/horn; B.H. Jackson, *Recollections of Sir Thomas Graham Jackson*, 117; information from Mrs Jane Barbour, Winchester.

A Dignity of Rectors
WESTON SUPER MARE,
St John the Evangelist

~◦✕◦~

Pevsner thought all Weston's churches were 'emphatically second in order of interest' to the terraces, hotels and other buildings which transformed the little fishing village into the genteel resort 'super Mare'. 'Churchgoer', visiting in 1845 to sample a sermon, thought St John's, then the only church in the place, 'one of the most raw, wretched, discreditable specimens of Christian architecture' he had ever seen.

The 'designer' of the building, or rather of the nave and tower which replaced the nave and tower of the late-medieval church, was evidently Richard Parsley, a Yorkshireman who was the largest tenant farmer and steward of the Pigott family of Brockley, owners of Weston since 1696. Thomas Pigott, founder of the family fortunes, had held lucrative government office in Ireland under Charles I and bought Brockley at the Restoration. His son John bought Weston and died in 1727. His son, also John, married the co-heir of the Ashton Court estate and was succeeded by his nephew John Bigg Pigott. Four brothers all managed to die without children, the last the Revd Wadham Pigott in 1823. In his lifetime he gave £1000 towards the new nave and tower, and at his death left the interest on £200 to be distributed in bread and meat at Christmas.

The development of Weston as a resort turned the flat moorland behind the sand dunes into valuable residential and commercial properties and the bare, sheep-grazed slopes of Weston Hill into desirable, leafy villa sites. The town became the summer home of many a prosperous Bristol family and a place of permanent retirement for East India Company folk. Such people, 'Churchgoer' found, crowded out the natives in the season, giving the church congregation a rather foreign air, almost like Calcutta cathedral.

The rebuilding of the church in 1824 was occasioned both by the need to replace a structure much out of repair (bundles of hay were stuffed into holes in the windows), and also to provide seating for more people. £800 were raised for the rebuilding by the sale of pews, many of them to keepers of local lodging houses. A gallery on three sides of the wide new nave brought the total sittings to 1000. The tiny old chancel and a chapel on its north side which served as a vestry room were retained until 1837 but still, 'Churchgoer' suspected, the chancel was deliberately kept small and cluttered to ensure that nothing like Tractarianism ('the most ingenious processionist') could ever be practised. The east window was filled with glass from a collection given by Bishop Law, the rector's father, and worth £500. The north aisle was added in 1844, probably thanks to the generosity of the same rector, and the 'useful but ugly' porch west of the tower in 1853.

168

Weston super Mare: *general view, 1829*

Weston was anti-Tractarian in 1845 and Pusey verging on anti-Christ if the opinions of the lady who spoke to 'Churchgoer' were typical. It had not always been so: the parish still held church ales in 1699, long after they had been suppressed by puritans elsewhere. To 'Churchgoer's' surprise the service in 1845 was decorous, the singing hearty, the sermon 'earnest and persuasive, though moderate and modest'. The singing had been revived by Stephen Jenkins, who succeeded Wadham Pigott as resident curate in 1823.

The modest preacher in 1845 was the Revd J.H. Forsyth, one of the two curates employed by the then rector, himself, it was said, unable to take services for the past three years because of ill health. As Weston the growing town was under the influence of the Pigotts, Weston the parish was the creature of successive bishops of Bath and Wells, the patrons of the living. Frederick Beadon, appointed in 1806 by his episcopal distant cousin and promoted by him as prebendary in 1807 resigned Weston in 1811 and in the following year became a canon residentiary in Wells, where he lived until his death in 1879 at the age of 101. James Scott, Beadon's successor, and rector from 1811 to 1826, held another living in Hampshire which he evidently found more attractive. After him came Francis Blackburne, who held a parish in Yorkshire as well but came to Weston at least once, and then fatally, for he was drowned there in 1829. He was followed by William Barlow, already holder of a living in Canterbury which he retained with Weston and with the rectory of Coddington (Cheshire) and a canonry of Chester, whence the new patron, Bishop George Henry Law, had come in 1824. Barlow, it was later remembered, was strongly opposed to Dissenters and only buried a child of such a family after the intervention of the archbishop of Canterbury.

Barlow was followed in 1840 by the bishop's influential son Henry Law, the rector who was absent from Weston not because of ill health but because he was in charge of the diocese as Chancellor for his senile father and was also archdeacon of Wells. This busy man was one of the national leaders of the Evangelical party and continued as rector of Weston until his promotion to the deanery of Gloucester in 1862.

Weston could ill afford an absentee rector, although three separate parishes had been formed out of the original one to serve parts of the growing town. St John's remained, of course, the mother church and its rector continued to be a man of ecclesiastical consequence. Law was succeeded by another archdeacon, R.W. Browne of Bath, formerly a prebendary of St Paul's and Professor of Classical Literature at King's College, London. George Buckle, rector 1876–88, who succeeded Browne was a modest man who fathered a diocesan architect and an Editor of *The Times*, reseated the parish church and founded the Church Institute. As an undergraduate at Oxford he had gained a first in mathematics and each year wrote for the *Guardian* a report of the annual meeting of the British Association. For a year before he resigned Weston he had lived at Wells as a canon residentiary, but the parish, which now included All Saints church and a Mission Room, was in the care of four curates.

Buckle's three successors were Archdeacon E.A. Salmon (1888-98), Prebendary W.J.

Weston super Mare: *exterior*

Birkbeck (1898–9) and Charles Fane De Salis (1899-1911), already an assistant diocesan inspector of schools, who in 1911 was consecrated the first suffragan bishop of Taunton since the sixteenth century. The bishops of Bath and Wells chose only the best for Weston.

Churchgoer's Rural Rides; Diocesan Kalendars; Visitors' Hand-Book to Weston-super-Mare; B. Brown and J. Loosley, *The Book of Weston super Mare*; E.E. Baker, *Weston super Mare Village Jottings.*

The Expression of Intelligent Devotion
SHEPTON BEAUCHAMP, *St Michael*

Two priests, James Stratton Coles and his son Vincent Stuckey Stratton Coles, are the outstanding figures in the history of Shepton Beauchamp. The parish church, like most of its neighbours, dates largely from the fourteenth and fifteenth centuries but there are traces of a tower at the east end of the north aisle and of a chapel opposite, indicating a cruciform building of about 1300. A new and probably longer chancel was built and aisles added to the nave in the fourteenth century and those aisles were rebuilt and the tall and ornate west tower added a century later. The old tower was left until about 1550. The fan vault in the new tower bears the bat's-wing badge of the Daubeney family who probably lent or gave money for its building. The scars of the demolished north tower can still be seen.

After that date the history of the church followed a familiar pattern. One rector was deprived for being married, another was imprisoned as a Royalist, a third lived for nearly forty years in Devon. A succession of curates regularly said Mattins and Evensong in the eighteenth century and celebrated communion three or four times a year. One sermon each Sunday was the rule in 1815, two by 1827. When James Coles arrived as rector in 1836 there were only five regular communicants, for the bishop had held a confirmation in the area only once in seven years.

The Revd V. S. S. Coles

The new rector introduced hymns, frequent celebrations of the Communion, daily Mattins, sermons on weekdays, even coloured altar frontals. With a revived liturgy came education and the restoration of the church building. A Sunday school had been started just before James Coles arrived but he had something to do with a new schoolrom in 1838 and with a completely new Church school in 1856. His daughter Julia began night schools for boys and girls in 1868 where they could learn to

Shepton Beauchamp: *former clergy house*

read and write, to study the Bible and to learn the Catechism. In 1865 the church was restored, the south aisle widened and new vestries were added to the designs of G.E. Street. On Census Sunday 1851 the congregation numbered 129 in the morning and 184 in the afternoon with 85 and 86 children. The total population in the same year was 647.

In 1872 James Coles was succeeded by his son Vincent who had been trained in the Tractarian parish of Wantage in Berkshire. There were already societies of St Gabriel and St Stephen in the parish when he arrived and within a year he had founded a third, the Society of the Holy Innocents, to encourage girls to become weekly communicants. Their monthly meetings under the leadership of his sister Julia involved 'a little talk', cups of tea and an occasional outing or dance. Miss Coles was later to found St Michael's Home 'for the reception of young girls who have fallen' where training in laundry and housework was given. The Holy Innocents were often found work in service in suitable parishes in other parts of the country.

Stuckey Coles (as he was called; his mother's father was the wealthy Langport banker Vincent Stuckey) immediately introduced daily Evensong, weekly Communion services and confession when he came in 1872, and the bishop soon heard complaints that he used white vestments at the Eucharist. Two years later he built a clergy house for himself, the vicar of Barrington and visiting priests and students, where they dined together in a

173

Shepton Beauchamp: *tower vault*

large central hall and had an oratory with a great crucifix.

The Eucharist lay at the heart of Stuckey Coles's teaching, with separate preparation classes for each of the social groups in the parish: the wives of tradesmen could not meet with the wives of labourers. Early services before work, he believed, were the way to gain the heart of the labouring man. 'What hope is there of a man's being drawn to Holy Communion,' he wrote, 'by a Sunday attendance at a service like Evensong which is admirably adapted for the expression of intelligent devotion, but which has very little in it that can seize and kindle the best elements in the sluggish and unspiritual nature of an ignorant and sleepy man?' The meticulous records the rector kept enable his success to be followed during the eleven years he served at Shepton: Easter communicants between 176 and 216, Christmas communicants between 98 and 151. In 1881 the total population was 640.

Shepton was 'a model parish of the Catholic Revival' and it still retains something of that flavour through the influence of the patrons of the living, the Community of the Resurrection at Mirfield, to whom Stuckey Coles gave the advowson in 1913. His interests lay far beyond his parish for he was in demand as a preacher and leader of missions, but nearer to home he was in close touch with other Tractarian parishes including Hambridge, East Brent and, of course, Barrington where his former curate served as vicar. When he left Shepton Stuckey Coles became Principal of St Stephen's House, Oxford, where he trained men in his own tradition.

R.W. Dunning, 'Nineteenth-century parochial sources', *Studies in Church History* 11, ed D. Baker, 301–8 based on S.R.O. D/P/she. b 2/5/1, 2/5/7, 4/1/1, 9/1/1.

For God and Empire
WHITELACKINGTON, *St Mary*

⮞⬥⬤⬥⮜

The Church of England was the church of Empire, but not many churches in the county can boast such impressive Imperial connections as Whitelackington. The Speke family had left the adjoining manor house long before John Hanning Speke first served in the Punjab with the Indian army and then went to Africa to discover Lake Victoria and the headwaters of the Nile, but several of his ancestors lie buried within the church. Families who came after them, squires of Dillington recorded on the walls of their aisle, and the connections of two rectors memorialised in the chancel, provided soldiers and governors in many other parts of the world. And the simple obelisk standing proud outside the churchyard and above the distant village records the names of lesser folk who gave their no less valuable lives in two World Wars.

Vaughan Hanning Vaughan-Lee (died 1882) in his youth fought in the Crimea with the 21st Royal North British Fusiliers but came home safely, and his son Arthur rose to be Colonel of his regiment, the Royal Horse Guards (the Blues). But William Stuart Northcote Johnson, grandson of a former vicar, fell at Aulnay near Loos attached to the 158th Regiment of French Infantry in October 1914; and John Arnold Buckland, elder son of the vicar and a 2nd Lieutenant in the Somerset Light Infantry, was also killed in France in March 1917 at the age of twenty.

Another former vicar had a happier pride in his sons. In 1825 Francis Charles Johnson was appointed to Whitelackington by his father Charles, prebendary of Whitelackington in Wells cathedral and patron of the living. He did not immediately come to the parish and for some time employed as his curate the young Charles Paul, from a landowning family in St Vincent in the West Indies. Charles Paul married Frances Kegan Horne, also from St Vincent, whose Uncle Kegan had earlier found himself the guardian of a boy named James Brooke. Frances was 'almost brought up' by her uncle with James, and James's sister married Francis Charles Johnson.

Paul's son Charles Kegan Paul, later a publisher, remembered James on his return from his first Indian expedition, for he 'was full of that charm which drew to him so many young men in his adventurous life'. For James was none other than that great Imperial character Sir James Brooke, Kt., K.C.B., D.C.L. (1803–68), first rajah of Sarawak, British commissioner and consul-general of Borneo, governor of Labuan.

James Brooke was unmarried, and he looked for a successor in Sarawak to his nephews, to two sons of Francis Johnson. He first turned to the eldest, John Brooke Johnson, who as designated heir assumed the name of Brooke. Formerly a captain in the 88th

Regiment of Foot, he became the second rajah but disappointed his uncle in his method of government and was replaced by his next brother Charles. Uncle and eldest nephew both died in 1868, and John's body lies in Whitelackington churchyard.

Charles Anthony, G.C.M.G., born at Berrow and the second Johnson son, then assumed the name Brooke. He had joined the Navy and first went out to Sarawak in 1852. He remained as rajah until 1916. There is no trace of him at Whitelackington although he had lived there as a boy. His next brother William Frederic (1830–1916) was a Royal Navy captain and lies in the churchyard. The youngest son was Henry Stuart, who also served in Sarawak under Sir James Brooke but returned to England because of poor health. He subsequently became deputy governor of Parkhurst and later of Chatham gaols and finally became chief constable of Edinburgh. He died in 1894. It was his son who fell at Aulnay in 1914. One of the two Johnson daughters to survive to adulthood was married to Gilbert Nicholetts, Colonel (so the tombstone reads) of the 2nd Beloochees Regiment – presumably the Baluchistan Regiment.

India, the West Indies, France and the Far East, so far the Empire spread; so far from home sons fought and died. Home, where Speke and Brooke and Johnson and Vaughan-Lee had worshipped, was never more English; and in one sense almost homely, for the curved-out arms and turned legs of the pews in the church could belong to any drawing room. For the rest, the nave tells the usual Somerset story of prosperity even here in the late fifteenth century, when it was heightened and widened leaving the mark of the earlier and lower roof-line above the tower arch and embracing the eastern buttresses of the tower.

The transepts belong to the early fourteenth century, both once chapels (hence the piscinae) and that on the south larger and incorporating a fine late-medieval crocketed niche. The north transept contains the flamboyant tomb Sir George Speke (died 1582) prepared for himself, perhaps many years before his death. In the same aisle is a modest memorial to the last male representative of his branch of the family, another George Speke (1690–1753), whose daughter Anne brought her husband Frederick occasionally to Dillington. Frederick can hardly be said to have shared the Whitelackington concept of Empire, for he was Frederick, Lord North, the man whose policy towards the American colonies drove them to independence from their mother country.

C.K. Paul, *Memories; Dictionary of National Biography*; memorials in the church and churchyard.

MIDSOMER NORTON,
St John the Baptist

᠇ᡃᡙᢉᠵ

O n Friday 13 September 1775 the Revd Mr Wesley applied to use the church at
Midsomer Norton and to his surprise the vicar not only 'cheerfully granted' his
request but actually sat in the congregation to hear him. That was not the normal reaction in the parishes of the Mendip coalfield but Edward Ford evidently had more
sympathy with Wesley than most of his fellow clergy.

That remarkable service took place in an ancient building the most recent part of which
was the west tower, erected in 1674 possibly through the generosity of the rich Sir
Charles Harbord, native of the parish, M.P. for Launceston and holder of a number of
lucrative government posts. Only that tower and some fragments formerly in the

Midsomer Norton: *exterior, 1995*

grounds of the Vicarage still remain from a church whose round-headed and zigzag-decorated doorways (of the same date as the surviving font) indicate a Norman building altered in the Decorated period.

The rectory, the church estate with the right to appoint a vicar, belonged for two centuries and more before the Dissolution to the Augustinian canons of Merton in Surrey – hence the old name Norton Canonicorum. The more recent name recalls the dedication festival of the church, the Birth of John the Baptist, 24 June, Midsummer Day. Ever since 1546 the patrons and owners of the rectory have been the dean and canons of Christchurch, Oxford.

The churchwardens' accounts of the eighteenth and early nineteenth centuries show a concern for the fabric of the church and for decent standards of behaviour. The building was regularly maintained and decorated with whitewash: in 1736 Joseph Maynard was paid for 'pinnacles and other things'; in 1739 a joiner and a plumber were busy and the church was ceiled; in 1754 'Mr Parsons (the architect)' was finally paid 'for new setting the south battlement'; in 1756 the whole building was rough cast 'and the sharp or poin [sic] end next the chancel taken down and rebuilt'; and in the same year Parsons and Robert Jones, a carpenter, were paid for designing and making a new pulpit in 'a decent and genteel manner'.

The pulpit may have been decent but behaviour in church left so much to be desired that in 1757 Richard Hawkins was paid 'for walking the church to observe decency during the time of Divine Service'. There was still an echo of that when at the Easter Vestry in 1893 concern was expressed at the unruly behaviour of youths in the gallery. Earlier, the gallery had been the place from which the singers led worship until 1816 when an organ by Nicholls of London was bought by public subscription headed by the handsome sum of £25 from the lord of the manor, no less than the Prince Regent himself. The total cost was just over £259 and a gallon of beer for labourers. The parish was already interested in music.

Ten years later and the wardens began to spend again. Perry and Row of Bath were paid for painting and varnishing the furnishings and for providing what was curiously described as 'a set of new commandments', presumably boards to be placed in the chancel rather than some sort of radical theology. The varnish did not last long, for in 1828 Mr Armstrong of Bristol and Mr Lewis of Bath each surveyed the building, Mr Smith of Bristol dismantled and crated the organ, unnamed craftsmen salvaged doors and took down memorials and parapets and an auctioneer was paid to sell unwanted materials. In place of the old church a new one arose to the design of John Pinch of Bath. The accounts are tantalisingly silent after the cost of laying the foundation stone in October 1828 until James Parfitt was paid 'on account of the New Church', and then in 1830 the organ blower was at work again. The new church was evidently finished and in use but the last bill was not paid until 1834, and not until a year later were the boundary walls, pillars and gates completed.

Midsomer Norton: *tower*

So much for the evidence of the parish records. Other sources confirm that the church was consecrated in 1832 and that the cost of over £4000 found subscribers in the Church Building Society (£500), the duchy of Cornwall (£300), the dean and chapter of Christchurch, Oxford (£100), and the Roman Catholic college (later abbey) at Downside (£50).

The new building had seats for 322 people but the population in 1831 was 2942 and rising. Pinch's design, in a vaguely Perpendicular style, produced a typical preaching house dominated by a central pulpit and desk placed in front of the chancel steps, the desk seven and the pulpit ten steps above contradiction. Galleries, of course, were absolutely necessary, but still the village expanded and by 1871 the population had risen to over 4000. Thus in 1875 Richard Gane of London, partner of C.E. Giles, produced a plan which provided more seats in the existing nave, provided a new chancel to the east of Pinch's chancel and a choir vestry on its north side. The dominant pulpit was to be demolished, the original chancel furnished with stalls for a choir and the new chancel stepped to form a spacious sanctuary. The character of the building, presumably reflecting the views of the vicar and his leading parishioners, had moved from Evangelicalism to something approaching Ritualism.

In the event Gane's plans proved too expensive for the parish but the determination to build a chancel and choir vestry was not forgotten. The re-ordered church seating 700 was opened in 1878 and worship was led for the first time by a cassocked and surpliced choir. Twenty years later the Easter Vestry was told of the generous gift of a new white altar cloth whose superfrontal had been the gift and work of Mrs and Miss Waugh, grandmother and aunt of Evelyn and Alec Waugh. Dr Waugh complained about the disorderly youths at the same meeting, having already called attention more than once to 'the irregularity with which the curfew is tolled'.

In 1914 the new vicar, the Revd W.D. Walter Williams, felt impelled to offer himself as a forces chaplain, but his experience led him on his return to revive the plan to build a new chancel both as a thank offering to God and as a tribute to the 56 men of the parish who had given their lives in the fighting. By 1922 the fund stood at over £1500 and the foundation stone of the new work, designed by W.D. Caroe, was laid by the marquess of Bath in 1924. Only a little over a year later it was dedicated and was almost paid for. At the same time the galleries were reduced in size, a heating system installed, and the organ moved.

Walter Williams was clearly a great spiritual force in the parish in his twelve years' ministry between 1914 and 1926, and he was supported by two able churchwardens, Messrs C.H. Shearn and I.B. Holloway. The liturgy was at the heart of their work, a regular Sung Eucharist every Sunday morning led by quality organist and trained choir. The statistics of progress spoke eloquently: in 1914, 246 Easter communicants, in 1926, 376; in 1914 communicants on Palm Sunday 22, in 1926, 123. In 1914 there had been 80 Easter communicants at the iron mission church in Radstock Road; in 1926 there were 108 Easter communicants at St Barnabas's, Welton.

In 1914 the parish income was £396. In 1923 the vicar had made an impassioned plea that every live member of the congregation should join the free-will offering scheme to wipe out a debt of £61. By 1926 the income was £877, and during the twelve years of his ministry some £3000 had been spent on church building. It was an achievement which the modest man was somewhat embarrassed to record, but he felt the church council ought to know. His successor at the end of 1926 was a man of similar mould, and he and the wardens together were soon working to ensure the continuance of a curate at Welton and the appointment of two lay readers for the parish as a whole. Not to be entirely outdone in 1934 a group of ladies in the parish formed themselves into a committee to raise money to turn the east porch of the church into a Lady Chapel. Within two years they had entirely succeeded.

S.R.O. D/P/msn.; *Guardian and Radstock Observer* 18 April, 1924.

Missionaries Apostolic
STRATTON ON THE FOSSE,
St Benedict

~⚜~

The community of Benedictine monks moved from Acton Burnell in Shropshire into the elegant house named Mount Pleasant in Midsomer Norton's Downside tithing in 1814. Very soon, in spite of hostile legislation, they felt able to look beyond their own immediate members, and the servants they brought with them were joined by a few converts. As early as 1818 the first baptism took place in the front parlour of Mount Pleasant at the hands of the prior. Two years later it was not the prior but one of the junior members of the community, Dom Bede Polding, who officiated, possibly because he had been entrusted with the care of the Catholic community in the area.

That first 'missionary' duty was followed by Polding's foundation of a school for Catholics in Stratton village, the prelude to a greater task. In 1834, having already declined to serve in India, Polding was consecrated as bishop to serve as vicar apostolic in New Holland, in the south-east of the new land of Australia. In 1842 he became archbishop of Sydney and remained far away from Downside until his death in 1877.

Archbishop Polding

His work among the lay people of the district was taken up strongly when Dom Nicholas Kendall was formally appointed 'missionary apostolic'. For six years he served as parish priest of an area which stretched as far north-west as the mission chapel at Hillgrove near Chewton Mendip. Under him the Guild of St Gregory the Great was founded in 1841 'as a means of spiritual and temporal assistance to the men of the parish'. The Guild proved of vital importance to many families and remained in existence until 1949.

In 1844 Kendall left to serve for forty years in mission parishes in Worcestershire and Gloucestershire and was followed at Stratton by another missionary-in-the-making, Dom Charles Davis. He, like Polding, realised the value of a village school and commissioned

Charles Hansom to design a building which would provide schoolrooms on either side of a teacher's house, to be erected by the lay cemetery in Stratton village near the site of Polding's old school.

Perhaps the scheme was too expensive or ambitious, perhaps Fr Davis's appointment as bishop of Maitland, New South Wales, and coadjutor to Dr Polding came too soon for its completion. He was undoubtedly founder of the school, but the building was perhaps only half finished when he left for the Antipodes in 1848. Nearly ten years were to elapse before the other half of Hansom's building was finished and by that time it had been transformed by the parish priest, Dom Alphonsus Morrall, into the parish church of St Benedict. It was opened in 1857.

Dom Alphonsus, who served for two years (1866–8) as prior of Downside, himself returned to the home mission field at Cheltenham and elsewhere from 1868 to 1888. He was followed as parish priest at Stratton (1859-62) by Dom Roger Bede Vaughan, another towering figure in the Empire Church. In 1873 he was appointed archbishop and coadjutor with right of succession to Dr Polding, and in 1877 he succeeded him as metropolitan of Australia. He died in Liverpool in 1883 on his way to Rome, aged only forty-nine.

Abbot Horne

Vaughan's immediate successors in the parish could hardly compete with such fame, but two priests, missionaries in their own distinctive ways, served the parish between them for eighty-four years. Dom Ethelbert Horne was appointed in 1891 and is still vividly remembered. As an antiquarian he wrote with authority on local scratch dials and dovecots, on medieval embroidery and holy wells; as an archaeologist his work on the Anglo-Saxon cemetery at Camerton achieved national recognition in his election to the fellowship of the Society of Antiquaries of London. His willing collaboration, wide interests and extraordinary energy made him the vital colleague of such figures as Dr Arthur Bulleid at the Meare lake village and Dean Armitage Robinson at Glastonbury abbey. His services to Somerset archaeology are reflected in his occupation of offices in the county archaeological society – chairman of council 1927–40, editor 1926-9, president 1940–2 – and it was entirely appropriate that having served his own community as prior from 1929 to 1934 he should have become titular abbot of Glastonbury, whose remains he had done so much to reveal and preserve.

Dom Ethelbert is also remembered in the parish at Stratton, a man 'widely respected and regarded with affection by all denominations', the 'father figure' of the village whose sons recalled painful visits to the sacristy table after some misdemeanour at school and whose lads recall the figure standing outside the village reading room daring Catholics to enter on a Sunday or to play cards there. Still alive from his time, too, is the village branch of the British Legion, so closely associated with St Benedict's.

Like Polding and Morrall before him Dom Ethelbert paid much attention to the school and his invitation in 1897 to Servite sisters to live and teach there benefited the whole village from the first through adult night classes in geography and needlework. A few fragmentary papers from the parish in his early days include accounts for 1894 showing a large financial loss (£40 12s) on the school but a respectable surplus (£29 5s 11d) on the church account from generous offertories (£29 8s) and bench rents (£29 17s 6d). Entirely typical Horne activities were the use of the bathing place on Mogg Hill for members of the reading room and a parish pilgrimage in 1893 to St Aldhelm's well at Doulting.

Dom Ethelbert's physical contribution to St Benedict's was notable, for in his time it was both enlarged and given what was for years its dominant feature. The original church had a spire on its north tower. In 1913 the nave was lengthened, the spire removed and other alterations made. In 1915 the magnificent decorated rood screen and reredos were installed, designed by Dom Ephram Seddon and made by William Chivers. The original statues of the reredos came from Italy and Dom Ethelbert added two more with local connections – the Blessed Richard Whiting, last abbot of Glastonbury, and St Vigor, patron saint of the Anglican parish church. On the top of the screen in ostrich-egg receptacles were relics of St Francis de Sales and St Philip Neri; the bishop of Bayeux and the church of Arras gave Dom Ethelbert some relics of St Vigor.

Some of the great screen was removed in 1957, part of what came to be a radical re-ordering of St Benedict's by a parish priest of a very different stamp. As a young monk in the 1930s Dom Gregory Murray was one of the greatest organists in the country. He came to be parish priest at Stratton in 1952 after long study in other disciplines and parish work in London and Lancashire. He is still fondly remembered for his direct and straightforward preaching and his deep knowledge of scripture; and he has left behind simple congregational music for vernacular settings of the Mass and hymns and psalm responses. His other legacy is the not entirely popular re-ordering of St Benedict's in the light of the Second Vatican Council. Adopting with enthusiasm the designs of Martin Fisher of Bath he removed what remained of Dom Ephram Seddon's screen and introduced a massive free-standing stone altar. It was entirely appropriate that part of the screen is preserved as the front of the organ loft.

Stratton on the Fosse: *St Benedict's church exterior*

The memorials in the burial ground on the east and south of St Benedict's record both English and foreign names, titled and undistinguished, many of them redolent of English Catholicism. Among them lies all that is mortal of Baron Friedrich von Hugel, the son of an Austrian father and a Scottish mother who lived as a child in Belgium and as an adult in England. His remarkable education at the hands of a Catholic historian, a Protestant pastor and a Quaker geologist produced, in the words of a distinguished dean of St Paul's, 'our greatest theologian and the ablest apologist for Christianity in our time'; another missionary apostolic.

Downside MSS. including an MS. history of the church by Gerald Brine; Norbert Birt, *Obit Book of the English Benedictines, 1600–1912*; *Proc. Som. Arch. Soc.* xcvii. 193–4; *Downside Review* Apr. 1992, 159–60.

Grappling with Finances
ANGERSLEIGH,
St Michael and All Angels

~✢~

The tiny church holds only eighty people and the parish, one of the smallest in the diocese, has ten houses and about forty people. The Romanesque font points to a church established not too long after the Norman Conquest, not necessarily the first building on the site midway down the slope between scattered farms and the hamlet of Lowton. The west tower was built in the fourteenth century, the nave in the years just before the Reformation. Some of the furnishings are much more modern: the carved oak panel and reredos (1913) were designed by Frederick Bligh Bond, and the carved bench ends, the west screen and the pulpit panels (1903–6) were the work of the remarkable man who for forty-six years from 1900 lived in Leigh Court next door to the church and for all that time was both patron of the living and rector's warden.

Arthur Edgell Eastwood (1859–1949) 'was greatly loved by those friends who knew him best' (so ran his obituary) and 'his greatest interest was in the affairs of the Church'. That

Arthur Eastwood

interest led him to be chosen as one of the first members of the Church Assembly and he played a leading part in the creation of the financial organisations of both the Central and the Diocesan Boards of Finance. No one understood better than he both the needs of the Church at diocesan and national level, and none better than he the financial demands made on even the smallest parishes. And it was typical of the man that for years he served as treasurer of Angersleigh P.C.C. and that most of its minutes were recorded in his own distinctive handwriting.

Like many another parish at the beginning of the twentieth century, Angersleigh had no endowments from which to repair the building and maintain its worship. A harvest home dinner proposed by the rector in 1906, a fancy fair in 1908, a rummage sale and regular winter dance meetings in 1909, and socials during 1910 helped to keep church finances afloat and also supported local projects such as the rethatching of the village room. Demands of the wider Church began to be made in 1914 when Angersleigh, like every other parish, was asked to contribute towards diocesan and national funds: the parish quota, as it was called, amounted to £3 6s 1d, a sum which could not be found from regular funds. It was therefore resolved to adopt a free will offering scheme, members of the congregation contributing 1d a week, with a special collection in church to cover any deficit. The people of Angersleigh rose magnificently to the occasion: in six months they had raised £5 8s 11d.

A special sale of work planned for that summer was abandoned because of the outbreak of war and the parish managed to survive without extra efforts until 1921 when a deficit of £18 was declared. Part of the problem was that the 15 subscribers to the free will offering had dwindled to seven 'and it was important,' the secretary recorded, 'that all members of the congregation should share in supporting the Church beyond the Parish.' The rector and Mr Eastwood were at one in their view, and a sale was proposed, to include stalls for jumble, new articles, produce and tea. No record of the sale has survived but not long afterwards the bells fell silent. Their repair was estimated to cost £90. So 'it was unanimously resolved' to hold a sale of work and gymkhana on Thursday (half-day closing) 20 July 1922.

In the event the gymkhana was perhaps forgotten in the rush of people to organise stalls: Mrs Pugh took on refreshments, Miss Bensant jumble, Mrs Hamilton provisions, Mr Eastwood miscellaneous (whatever that was), and Mrs Horspool, the rector's wife, the work party stall, the Sunday school stall and the rectory stall. The rector promised to try and find someone to arrange advertising. Amusements were planned to include guessing the name of a doll, hoop-la, Aunt Sally, a fortune teller and 'home of departed spirits'. The Norton Band was to be asked to play and there was to be dancing in the evening.

Such an effort was not possible, or even necessary, every year, but by the end of 1925 another deficit had to be cleared, the Rectory needed repairs, and a sick and poor fund was needed to help the new rector with families in trouble. By this time there was a noticeable weakening of the community spirit in the parish; there had been no support for the socials in the village room that winter because there were 'so many entertainments in adjoining parishes, to say nothing of the attractions of wireless'.

The March jumble sale brought people together and the fête on the last Thursday in May was a great success. The working party stall made nearly £15, the basket stall nearly £12, and skittles made £9 6s 6d thanks to the gift of the prize pig. Visitors guessed the weight of the cake and the number of pens in a bottle, identified scents, played clock golf, admired their own offerings on the produce stall and were a little ashamed of their cast-offs on the white elephant; children fumbled in bran and fished. There was dancing again in the evening, and a small outlay was recorded for the cost of a bus to bring the police, presumably to direct traffic rather than to prevent rowdyism.

Mr Eastwood had estimated that outlay for the year would amount to £50; the net profit was £58 16s 2d.

No similar effort was needed for several years after that. In 1931 over £29 was raised and spent immediately; in 1935 members of the Mothers' Union were made responsible for the cost of repairs to the east end of the chancel; a skittles week arranged between hay and harvest (a pig, a goose, a cheese and 5s offered as prizes) had to be dropped because heavy rain put back haymaking by almost a month. A jumble sale in 1937 was organised not for the church (accounts were satisfactory) but partly for the village room fund, partly for the hospital apple tree.

A great effort was proposed for the summer of 1939. Everyone knew it was something of a risk. The date was set for 13 July at the rectory but, because of the wet weather again, was postponed to 24 August at Leigh Court. Dean Bennett began with prayers 'because of the grave and critical condition of the political situation' before Mrs Barrett opened proceedings with a few well chosen words. The net result was £35 17s 4d. Perhaps rather surprisingly the tea stall run by the Leigh Court staff made only £2 18s; Mrs Clements' beauty stall did rather better and the household stall did best of all. But late August 1939 was no time to have an enjoyable afternoon.

Among the consequences of five years of conflict was the increase in the diocesan quota by 50 per cent, but it was decided (was this Mr Eastwood's influence again?) 'not to appeal against it as being excessive for so small a Parish, but to endeavour as far as possible to meet it'. That remains the attitude of Angersleigh. Despite (or perhaps because of) its small size the parish is still able to face with confidence a future which many another is unable to contemplate because its annual summer fair has become famous for miles around. On the last Saturday in July 1993 stalls, sideshows, games, competitions, children's events and teas produced the sum of over £1967. Each year the support is the same if not greater. Harvest festival and carol singing raise yet more. Angersleigh's parish share, its contribution to the costs of the whole Church, is every year paid in full. And, if that were not enough, bellringers have led a campaign which in a year raised £15,000 for repairs and the addition of a bell to the ring. The congregation will not be depressed by a decaying building.

S.R.O. D/P/ang 4/1/1, 9/1/1; information from Mrs Jenny Aish.

An Adaptable Building
GALMINGTON,
St Michael the Archangel

T he growing congregation in the spreading south-Taunton suburb of Galmington were in many ways fortunate, although they might not have thought so when in 1969 their first church was declared unsafe and was demolished; and their second, because of planning regulations, was given but a short time to live. Yet a new site, an imaginative architect, a committee intent on a multi-purpose building, and faith, energy and commitment in ample measure produced in 1987 a third church, and a debt whose swift removal was something of a miracle.

Back in 1864 when the vicars of Wilton and Bishops Hull had together established a little day school, the church had taken on a community role in the tiny farming hamlet. The school proved, in fact, a failure but the room was also used for a Sunday school, for

Galmington: *interior of iron church*

189

mission services, for meetings of the Band of Hope and for political gatherings, and by 1886 regular Sunday services were being held there. After the first, corrugated-iron St Michael's church had been opened in 1892 the old schoolroom was used for social evenings and concerts, as a distribution centre for the local blanket charity and as headquarters for the Scouts. By the 1930s Guides and Brownies were there and a mens' club. By 1934, when the hamlet began to grow, the Sunday school numbered 70.

At the beginning of the Second World War the room was used as a dispersal point for evacuees and later as a billet for men who recovered crashed aircraft. Somehow the people managed without it and worship in the little church continued without a break. After the war plans emerged for building houses on the fields between Galmington and Taunton and church leaders had to consider the future. The old schoolroom was in regular use again for whist drives, sales, socials, Guides, Brownies, parties and the ping pong club; in fact, it was the social centre of the hamlet, but its condition was not good. Members of the congregation took the initiative and formed a supper club to raise funds for a new hall.

In face of the new homes going up, would not the Borough Council find a site more central for the growing community ? The answer was no, but an orchard next to the church became available and a prefabricated hall was opened there in 1962. It

Galmington: *interior of present church, 1995*

immediately became the home of a youth club and the playgroup, and the debt was cleared and a community was forged through Christmas bazaars, whist drives, skittles weeks and summer fêtes.

From 1969 the hall took on a new role, for the closure and later demolition of the iron church left it, for a short time, as a place of worship, too. Early in 1971 a structure was erected beside it which soon became a worship centre to which the hall served as an overflow. And in not many years it was regularly in use, for the ministry of a resident curate and much new building brought people to church in greater numbers.

But the church was from the beginning a temporary structure and the planners gave notice that its licence to survive would expire in 1987. Meanwhile the diocesan authorities talked of reorganisation in almost infinite variety. It was clear that hall and temporary church were hampering growth and were in the wrong place in the spreading community, but was it sensible to build a church alone ? John Fisher, resident curate from 1980, had the vision of a new church on a new site; his local committee caught that vision and eventually Stephen Bartleet was commissioned to translate it into what the old schoolroom and the prefabricated hall had been for so long, coupled with what the two churches of St Michael had come to offer and to be.

The result, much nearer the physical heart of the community on a site bought almost at the last minute, was dedicated in the name of St Michael the Archangel in June 1987. Some have described it as a tithe barn in concept, and under its main roof is a central space which is wide nave and sanctuary with screens each side which can be drawn back to bring in the whole width of the building or drawn across to give separate rooms. Here is scope for traditional worship in altar-facing seats or worship in the round. In its short life the building has been a theatre for pantomime, a hall for bazaars, a meeting room for PCCs; meals have been eaten there, games played there, concerts enjoyed there. Parts have been used by local clubs, by the playgroup and other church organisations. But it remains, for all that, much more than a hall; it is the worship centre of the community.

R. Dunning, *A Goodly Heritage: the story of St Michael's, Galmington, 1864–1992.*

Bibliography

MANUSCRIPTS:

Somerset Record Office, Obridge Road, Taunton:

Bath and Wells Diocesan Records:

Many references made to the state of churches in 1547, 1554, and 1557 are not given specific sources. They are the diocesan visitation Act Books, which are to be found under the code D/D/Ca 17, 22, 27.

Bishops' Registers (D/D/B reg) 38, register of Bishop Lord Auckland (1854-69).

Faculty Papers (D/D/Cf).

Faculty Petitions (D/D/C pet).

Parish Records (D/P/): Angersleigh (ang).

Cameley (cmly).

Charlton Musgrove (ch.mu).

East Coker (cok.e).

Hornblotton (horn).

Midsomer Norton (msn).

Oare (oare).

Shepton Beauchamp (she.b).

Wells, St Cuthbert (wells st.c).

Nonconformist Records (D/N/):

Frome Methodist Circuit (fr.c).

Taunton, Mary Street Chapel (tau. mst).

Deposited Documents (DD/):

Poulett MSS. DD/PT.

Somerset Archaeological Society, DD/SAS, Wedlake Papers.

Trollope-Bellew MSS. DD/TB.

Wells Cathedral Library:

Liber Ruber.

Public Record Office, Chancery Lane, London:

Chancery, Early Proceedings, C 1.

Exchequer, Augmentations Office, Miscellaneous Books, Miscellaneous Charters, E 315.

–, ––, Ancient Deeds Series B, E 326.

PRINTED SOURCES:

English Episcopal Acta, X: Bath and Wells, 1061–1205, ed. F.M.R. Ramsey (British Academy, 1995).

Calendar of the Register of John de Drokensford ... 1309-29, ed. E. Hobhouse (Somerset Record Society i, 1887).

The Survey and Rental of the Chantries, Colleges and Free Chapels ... in the County of Somerset ... 1548, ed. E. Green (Somerset Record Society ii, 1888).

Churchwardens' Accounts of Croscombe, Pilton, Yatton, Tintinhull, Morebath and St Michael's,

Bath, ed. E. Hobhouse (Somerset Record Society iv, 1890).

The Register of Ralph of Shrewsbury, Bishop of Bath and Wells 1329-63, ed. T.S. Holmes (Somerset Record Society ix–x, 1896).

The Registers of Walter Giffard, 1265-6, and Henry Bowett, 1401-7, Bishops of Bath and Wells, ed. T.S. Holmes (Somerset Record Society xiii, 1899).

Somerset Medieval Wills, 1383–1500, ed. F. W. Weaver (Somerset Record Society xvi, 1901).

Somerset Medieval Wills, 1501–30, ed. F. W. Weaver (Somerset Record Society xix, 1903).

Somerset Medieval Wills, 1531–8, ed. F. W. Weaver (Somerset Record Society xxx, 1905).

The Register of Nicholas Bubwith, Bishop of Bath and Wells 1407-24, ed. T.S. Holmes (Somerset Record Society xxix–xxx, 1914).

The Register of John Stafford, Bishop of Bath and Wells 1425-43, ed. T.S. Holmes (Somerset Record Society xxxi–xxxii, 1915–16).

The Life of Richard Kidder, D.D., Bishop of Bath and Wells, ed. A.E. Robinson (Somerset Record Society xxxvii, 1924).

The Register of Thomas Bekynton, Bishop of Bath and Wells 1443-65, edd. H. C. Maxwell–Lyte and M. C. B. Dawes (Somerset Record Society xlix and l, 1934–5).

The Registers of Robert Stillington (1466-91) and Richard Fox (1492-4), Bishops of Bath and Wells, ed. H. C. Maxwell-Lyte (Somerset Record Society lii, 1937).

The Registers of Oliver King (1496-1503) and Hadrian de Castello (1503-18), Bishops of Bath and Wells, ed. H. Maxwell-Lyte (Somerset Record Society liv, 1939).

The Registers of Thomas Wolsey (1518-23), John Clerke (1523-41), William Knyght (1541-7), and Gilbert Bourne (1554-9), Bishops of Bath and Wells, ed. H.C. Maxwell-Lyte (Somerset Record Society lv, 1940).

Stogursey Charters, edd. T. D. Tremlett and N. Blakiston (Somerset Record Society lxi, 1949).

Medieval Deeds of Bath and District, edd. B. R. Kemp and D. M. M. Shorrocks (Somerset Record Society lxxiii, 1974).

The Somersetshire Quarterly Meeting of the Society of Friends 1668-99, ed. S. C. Morland (Somerset Record Society lxxv, 1978).

Calendar of Somerset Chantry Grants, 1548-1603, ed. G. H. Woodward (Somerset Record Society lxxvii, 1982).

Sir Stephen Glynne's Church Notes for Somerset, ed. M. McGarvie (Somerset Record Society lxxxii, 1994).

Churchwardens' Accounts, edd. R.W. Dunning and M.B. McDermott (Somerset Record Society lxxxiv, 1996).

Alfred the Great, trans. S. Keynes and M. Lapidge (Penguin Books, 1983).

Bath and Wells Diocesan Directory (1908 onwards).

The Bath and Wells Diocesan Kalendar (1888–1907).

Bede, *A History of the English Church and People*, trans. L. Sherley-Price (Penguin Books, Harmondsworth, 1955).

The Cartulary of Cirencester Abbey ed. C. D. Ross (Oxford University Press, 2 vols. 1964).

Calendar of the Manuscripts of the Dean and Chapter of Wells (Historical Manuscripts Commission, 2 vols. 1907, 1914).

The Churchgoer [J. Leech], *Being a Series of Visits to the Various Churches of Bristol* (Bristol, 1845).

The Churchgoer [J. Leech], *Rural Rides; or Calls at Country Churches* (Bristol, Series 1 (1847) and 2 (1851)).

The Church Rambler (Bath Herald, 2 vols. 1876).

English Historical Documents i, c. 500–1042, ed. D. Whitelock (Eyre Methuen, 2nd edn. 1979).

J. Leland, *Itinerary*, ed. L. T. Smith (reprinted Centaur Press, 5 vols., 1964).

J. Le Neve, *Fasti Ecclesie Anglicane, 1300–1541*, ed. B. Jones (Institute of Historical Research, 1964).

J. Le Neve, *Fasti Ecclesie Anglicane, 1541–1857*, edd. J. M. Horn & D. S. Bailey (Institute of Historical Research, 1979).

Somerset Protestation Returns and Subsidy Rolls, edd. A.J. Howard and T.L. Stoate (Almondsbury, 1975).

J. Skinner, *Journal of a Somerset Rector, 1822–32*, edd. H. Coombs and A. N. Bax (John Murray, 1930).

J. Skinner, *Journal of A Somerset Rector, 1803–34*, edd. H. and P. Coombs (Oxford University Press, 1971).

F. W. Weaver (ed.), *Somerset Incumbents* (Bristol, privately printed, 1889).

The Wells Miscellany, iv (June 1854).

Willelmi Malmesbiriensis Monachi de Gestis Pontificum Anglorum, Libri Quinque, ed. N. E. S. A. Hamilton (Rolls Series 52, London, 1870).

J. Woodforde, *The Diary of a Country Parson 1758–1802*, selected and ed. J. Beresford (Oxford University Press, 1978).

SECONDARY SOURCES:

W.H. Askwith, *The Church of St Mary Magdalene, Taunton* (Taunton, Phoenix Press, 1908).

E.E. Baker, *Weston super Mare Village Jottings* (1911).

T. G. Barnes, *Somerset 1625–40* (Oxford University Press, 1961).

J. Batten, *Historical and Topographical Collections relating to the Early History of Parts of South Somerset* (Whitby, Yeovil, Simpkin, Marshall & Co., London, 1894), reprinted as *Batten's South Somerset Villages* (Somerset Books, 1994)

P. Belham, *The Making of Frome* (Frome Society for Local Study, 1973).

F. Bennett, *The Story of W. J. E. Bennett...* (Longmans, Green & Co., 1909).

W. J. E. Bennett, *Pastoral Letter to the Parishioners of Frome* (Frome, 1852)

W. J. E. Bennett, *History of the Old Church of St John of Froome* (W. C. and J. Penny, Frome; Whittaker & Co., London, 1866).

J. H. Bettey, *Wessex from AD 1000* (Longmans, 1986).

H. N. Birt, *The Obit Book of the English Benedictines, 1600–1912* (Edinburgh, privately printed, 1913).

B. Brown and J. Loosley, *The Book of Weston super Mare* (Barracuda Books, Buckingham, 1979).

C. M. Church, *Chapters in the Early History of the Church of Wells* (Eliot Stock, 1894).

L. Cochrane, *Adelard of Bath: the First English Scientist* (British Museum Press, 1994).

G. E. Cockayne and others, *Complete Peerage* (13 vols in 12, St Catherine Press, 1910–59).

J. Collinson, *The History and Antiquities of the County of Somerset* (Bath, 1791).

J. Coombs, *George Anthony Denison* (London, 1984).

J. Cottle, *Some Account of the Church of St Mary Magdalene, Taunton* (1845).

R. Custance (ed.), *Winchester College, Sixth-Centenary Essays* (Oxford University Press, 1982).

[S.] Cuzner, *Cuzner's Hand-Book to Froome-Selwood* (Frome, 1866).

D. Dales, *Dunstan: Saint and Statesman* (Lutterworth Press, 1988).

R. W. Dunning, 'The Muniments of Syon Abbey', *Bulletin of the Institute of Historical Research* xxxvii (1964), 103–11.

R. W. Dunning, *The Church of St George, Beckington* (Beckington Parochial Church Council, 1973).

R. W. Dunning, 'Nineteenth-century Parochial Sources', *Studies in Church History* 11, ed. D Baker (Ecclesiastical History Society, 1975, 301–8.

R. W. Dunning, (ed.), *Christianity in Somerset* (Somerset County Council, 1976).

R. W. Dunning, 'The Minster at Crewkerne', *Proc. Som. Arch. Soc.* cxx (1976), 63–7.

R. W. Dunning, *The Monmouth Rebellion* (Dovecote Press, 1984)

R. W. Dunning, 'The West-Country Carthusians', *Religious Belief and Ecclesiastical Careers in Late Medieval England,* ed. C Harper-Bill (Boydell Press, 1991), 33–42.

R. W. Dunning, *Bridgwater, History and Guide* (Alan Sutton Publishing, 1992).

R. W. Dunning, *A Goodly Heritage. The Story of St Michael's, Galmington, 1864–1992* (privately printed, 1992).

R. W. Dunning, *Glastonbury, History and Guide* (Alan Sutton Publishing, 1994).

R. W. Dunning, with B. Fletcher and I. Burrow, *St Hugh of Witham and his Priory* (1986).

A.B. Emden, *A Biographical Dictionary of the University of Oxford to 1500* (Oxford University Press, 3 vols. 1957–74).

W.F. Emons-Nijenhuis, The Vision of Edmund Leversedge (Doctoral thesis, Catholic University of Nijmegen, 1990).

D.H. Farmer, *The Oxford Dictionary of Saints* (Clarendon Press, 1978).

J. H. Harvey, 'The Church Towers of Somerset', *Transactions of the Ancient Monuments Society,* 26 (1982), 157–83.

J. H. Harvey, *English Medieval Architects: a biographical dictionary down to 1550* (revised edition, Alan Sutton, 1984).

J Hurley, *Exmoor in Wartime, 1939–45* (Exmoor Press, 1978).

E.E. J[arrett], *History of St Peter's Church, Camerton* (Bath, 1892).

[W. King] Lord Bishop of Rochester, *An Account of the Marble Altar Piece Placed in ... the Parish Church of Burnham* (Bath, 1826).

M. D. Knowles, *The Monastic Order in England* (Cambridge University Press, 1950).

P. Leach, *Shepton Mallet: Romano-Britons and Early Christians in Somerset* (Birmingham University Field Archaeology Unit and Showerings Limited, 1991).

H. C. Maxwell Lyte, *A History of Dunster* (St Catherine Press, 2 vols., 1909).

M. McGarvie, *Light in Selwood* (Frome Society for Local Study, 1976).

M. McGarvie, *Witham Friary, Church and Parish* (Frome Society for Local Study, 1981).

H.P. Palmer, *Joseph Wolff* (Heath Cranton, 1935).

C.K. Paul, *Memories* (1899, reprinted Routledge & Kegan Paul, 1971).

N. B. Pevsner, *North and West Somerset* (Penguin Books, Harmondsworth, 1958).

N. B. Pevsner, *South and West Somerset* (Penguin Books, Hardmonsworth, 1958).

E. H. Plumptre, *The Life of Thomas Ken* (Isbister, London, 2 vols., 1890).

H. M. Porter, *Saint Aldhelm, Abbot and Bishop* (privately printed, 1978).

S. W. (Mrs C. W. H.) Rawlins, *Members of Parliament for the County of Somerset* (Taunton, Somersetshire Archaeological Society, 1939).

S. W. (Mrs C. W. H.) Rawlins, *The Sheriffs of Somerset* (Taunton, Somersetshire Archaeological Society, 1968).

J. A. Robinson, *Somerset Historical Essays* (British Academy, 1921).

L. F. Salzman, *Building in England down to 1540* (Oxford University Press, reprinted 1967).

I. J. Sanders, *English Baronies* (Oxford University Press, 1960).

T. Serel, *Historical Notes on the Church of St Cuthbert in Wells* (Wells, 1875).

S. Tuck, *Wesleyan Methodism in Frome* (Frome, 1837).

G. L. Turner (ed.), *Original Records of Early Nonconformity under Persecution and Indulgence* (Unwin, 3 vols., 1911–14).

The Victoria History of the County of Somerset, i and ii ed. W. Page (Constable and Co. 1906, 1911); iii–vi ed. R. W. Dunning (Oxford University Press, 1974, 1978, 1985, 1992).

Visitors' Handbook to Weston-super-Mare and its Vicinity, ed. L.E.H.J. (Weston, 1877).

J. C. Wedgwood with A. D. Holt, *History of Parliament: Biographies of Members of the House of Commons, 1439–1509* (H.M. Stationery Office, 1936).

A. K. Wickham, *Churches of Somerset* (Phoenix House, London 1952, new edition, David and Charles, Dawlish, 1965).

W. M. Wigfield, *The Monmouth Rebellion* (Moonraker Press, 1980).

C. Woodforde, *Stained Glass in Somerset 1250–1830* (Oxford University Press, 1946, reprinted Kingsmead Reprints, Bath, 1970).

Index

abb - abbot; abp - archbishop; archd - archdeacon; bp - bishop; bpric - bishopric; cath - cathedral; ch - church; preb - prebend(ary); rec - rector; s - super; vic - vicar

Cloos, John, rec of Tintinhull, 74
Cobbett, William, 135
Coddington, Ches, 169
Coker, East, ch, 139-42; rec, 139; vic, 139
Cole, Thomas, 61
Coleford, 136
Coles, James, Stratton, rec of Shepton Beauchamp, 156, 172-3; Julia, 172-3; Vincent Stuckey Stratton, rec of Shepton Beauchamp, 172-4
Colyns, Henry, 12
Colyton, Devon, 117
Combe St Nicholas, 44
communion tables, 104, 158
Compostella, Spain, 98
Compton, John, 102
Compton Martin, 33-5
confirmation, 147, 163, 172
Congregationalists, 24, 118-20
consecration, 156, 165, 180
Constance, council, 61
Coombes, Fr, 147, 149
Cornwall, duchy, 180
Cote, William, 12
Cotele, Elias, 149
Coumb, John, rec of Croscombe, 78
Countisbury, Devon, 127
Courtenay, Hugh, 1st earl of Devon, 139; family, 17, 139, 141
Coutances, France, bp, 132
Cox, Robert, 105; Robert, minister, 118
Crewkerne, Ashcombe, 14; ch, 12, 14-17; Eastham, 14; Henley, 14; rec, 56, and see Plummer, Samborne, Surland
Creyghton, Robert, precentor of Wells, 49; Robert, vic of Burnham, 49
Croscombe, ch, 76-9; rec, 79, and see Coumb
Cross, Squire, 130-1
Culbone, 126, 128
Curry, North, ch, 84-6; vic, 86
Curry Mallet, 85, 156
Cuthbert, St, 90
Cynegils, king, 5
Cynethrith, 18

Dales, Douglas, 18
Dampier, William, 142

Dane, John the, 29
Daubeney, family, 172
Davis, Dom Charles, priest of Stratton, bp of Maitland, 182-3; Lewis Charles, rec of Charlton Musgrove, 159
Decuman, St, viii, 1-2, 5
dedication, 46, 48, 52, 178
Delhi, India, 153
Denison, George, archd of Taunton, 154, 156, 161
Derry, bp, see Downham
Deverill, Wilts, 33
Dewlish, Dors, 154
Dillington, 175-6
Dinder, 98
Dissenters, 121, 163, 169
Dissolution, 24, 43, 64, 71, 75, 105, 108, 121, 178
Ditcheat, 159
Dodge, Nicholas, 142
Doone (Dune), Carver, 125; Sir Ensor, 125; Hugh, 126; Lorna, 125; Richard, 126; family, 127-8
Dorchester, Massachusetts, U.S.A., 118
Douai, France, 147
Doulting, viii, 5, 160, 167, 184
dovecot, 43, 71, 183
Downham, George, preb of Yatton, bp of Derry, 31
Downside, 40; abbey, 149, 180; prior, 182, and see Morrall; school, 40
Draycott, 99
Drokensford, John, bp of Bath and Wells, 29, 31, 47-8
Dromore, Ireland, bp, 154
Drummond, Henry, 153
Dublin, abp, see Inge; Trinity College, 154
Dunkeswell, Devon, abbey, 152
Dunstan, St, abb of Glastonbury, bp of Worcester, London, abp of Canterbury, 12, 18-21, 33, 44
Dunster, ch, 38, 67-71; monks, 70; prior, 68, 70-1, and see Childeston; priory, 68; vic, 68
Dyer, Capt John, 121; family, 121

Eadred, king, 19
Eastwood, A.E., 186-8

William, the Conqueror, 14, 29, 36, 67; II, 29; III, 124

Williams, W.D. Walter, vic of Midsomer Norton, 180-1; Mr, 141

Williton, 2

Wilton, 139; vic, 189

Wiltshire, Mrs Charity, 134

Wincanton, 159

Winchester, bp, see Alphege, Ethelwold; bpric, 18; College, 25, 102, 130

Winsham, 44

Witham Friary, 118-19; ch, 40-2

Wiveliscombe, 44, 56; dispensary, 49

Wolff, Lady Georgiana, 156; Joseph, vic of Isle Brewers, 153-4, 156

Wolsey, Thomas, cardinal, 143

Wood, John, the younger, architect, 132

Woodforde, James, curate of Thurloxton, 129- -31

Woolley, ch, 132-4; rec, see Grigg

Worcester, bp, see Dunstan, Ecguin; dean, see Hicks

Worgan, Matthew, 132

Wormleighton, Francis, artist, 167

Wren, Sir Christopher, architect, 49

Wrington, 114

Wulfric (of Haselbury), St, 34-5

Wyatt, James, architect, 146

Wyatville, Jeffry, architect, 146

Wyche, John, rec of Tintinhull, 74

Wyndham, John, 4; Sir John, 4; William, 4; Col, 61; family, 2, 4

Wynflaed, 54

Wynford, William, freemason, 57-8

Yatton, ch, 29-32, 44; preb, 29, 31, and see Downham, Nykke, Purveour, Taylour, Ward

Yeoman, Thomas, 119

Yeovil, rec, see More, Rissington, Samborne, Walerand; St John's ch, 54-8; provost, 55, 57; vic, 55, 57-8, and see Butler

Yewins, Richard, 118